A Business Approach to Personal Power

JARED A. CHAMBERS

Copyright © 2019 Chambers Creative Communication Concepts

All rights reserved.

ISBN: 978-0-578-51008-8

This book is intended to provide information to a general audience, and is not intended to provide specific legal, financial, or professional advice. No part of this book may be reproduced or transmitted in any form without express written permission of the author.

DEDICATION

This book is dedicated to anyone and everyone who's faced adversity, and in it found the strength and will to fight back to live life on purpose.

And, of course, my family, friends, and supporters who are too numerous to mention, without whom this effort would not have been possible.

CONTENTS

	Preface	i
1	Branding	1
2	Finance & Capital	8
3	Negotiation	16
4	Writing	27
5	Presentation	36
6	Technical Mastery	41
7	Process & Management	47
8	Real Life	52
	Afterword	62

PREFACE

"Why not me?" You see the examples of freedom, prosperity, and success all around.

You've asked the question. You still don't have an answer because you keep looking in the wrong place:

"I worked so hard!"

"I'm talented!"

"I'm smart!"

"I followed the rules!"

Frustrated that your affirmative case of doing exactly what you were supposed to do went nowhere, you make the negative case:

"They cheated!"

"They'd screw over their own mother!"

"I would never kiss ass like them!"

"It's not what you know, it's who you know!"

In your defense, it's all true.

To varying degrees, some or all of these statements are true, all of the time, in everything. They just don't answer your question, "Why not me?"

Any could be a factor in a given situation, but on average these reasons don't explain the disconnect between what you could be and what you actually are.

If you're willing to consider other answers, read on.

If you're not, close this book now. It gets uncomfortable.

Don't misunderstand—healthy skepticism and questions will actually help you read this book. There's a lot of conditioning we must shed. This is an active process of taking inventory and making plans. Still, there's no promise of foolproof success or that you can win a truly rigged game. Remember that great cinematic classic *WarGames*? Sometimes, "The only winning move is not to play."

Though philosophy students of Mick Jagger know that "*You Can't Always Get What You Want*," I start from the premise you CAN get more.

You just need to focus on areas in which you can win, and formulate a winning strategy. Fortunately, the business world offers a great model of how to do that, because that's exactly what a business must do. And really, how are you any different? You need to be cash positive, which means you need to not only have value to offer; you have to convince others that offer is valuable. Presumably, you'll be able to deliver on that with a degree of technical mastery, leveraging it into new opportunities.

But if you're interested in this book, you might've heard that "You're a business of one!" line before. A key point of differentiation is that many spouting that line think your focus should be on B2B (business-to-business) selling a single customer, which becomes your employer. Now, I've been in sales and marketing for two decades, and I'll let you in on an industry secret about single-customer businesses: *They all inevitably fail, which is usually a huge relief after working at an unsustainable level for very little reward.*

While the principles I will share will help you as an employee, I will consider this a failure if I don't get you to think bigger and more holistically. *Why* is always just as important as *how*. Speaking of holistic, I hope you're ready for something deeper than a *Forbes* or *Inc.* magazine listicle about discovering your inner influencer, too. "Be confident!" "Network!" "Be dependable!" Blah, blah, blah-bity, blah. You'd be as well off listening to 40-plus year old Steve Martin comedy bits intended as mockery of this sort of shallow self-help: "You! ...Can be a MILLIONAIRE!!! First, get a million dollars...."

Good qualities are the result of good systems built on good first principles. You already know what you want to be. You'd be that already if you could simply "Be!" Even if someone could tell you *how* to be, that's slightly more helpful but still lacking a foundation. You might get something from a step-by-step how-to, but it's never quite that simple—something the successful people writing them seem to forget after they've arrived at their destination.

You need to sit down in the boardroom as the CEO, with the COO, CFO, CBO, CMO, CSO, and CTO of Self, Inc., taking a departmental inventory, from which you can both build a strategy as well as figure out which tactical steps to execute. And when you do that, no one will need to tell you, "Be confident!" You will be. You'll find it easier to network. You'll be viewed as dependable. You will be perceived as professional. You will be more independent, and more free.

I've done that for myself. I've done it for companies and organizations. I've done it for friends. And I can do it for you, because, after all, why NOT you?

1 BRANDING

Who ARE you?

Just the chapter title is already triggering a bunch of you to respond with what you're not:

"I'm not a brand; I'm a person!"

Yeah, I get it. A bunch of grifters and hacks who hadn't landed a job on their own, without the help of their deep connections, in at least a dozen years tried to take a few good (and usually obvious) ideas about how to present yourself and turn it into a stand-alone genre of self-help materials called "personal branding." Too often, the ideas were actually *anti-branding*. Instead of how to build consistency and recognition around what's unique about you, it was more seven-item lists of how to be the most conforming, accommodating *you* possible.

So for those of you about to put up a huge wall, I understand—"help others" isn't a brand. But make no mistake; "Just be yourself" is equally atrocious advice, in spite of the ubiquity with which it is offered.

I want to kill both of those ideas here and now; creative destruction for the new foundation we are building. I will not talk about "helping others." I am not your mother. I am not your preacher. Helping others may be a virtue to them, but I do not expect your life to be a charity. I don't think that's cold, either: The more you can help yourself, the less charity is needed and the more it can be focused where it truly is. Instead, I will talk about the concept of *mutual benefit*.

In the same way, I can hardly ask you to be yourself when I don't know you and can't really comment on whether I even like you. Don't be mad—

how many people have you wanted to suggest, "Please, be different than yourself. Whatever you've been doing, just stop?" You can't please all the people all of the time, nor should you try. You should, however, probably do the math on the common denominator if every relationship equation in your life is divisible by exactly one YOU. So, let's instead talk about being *genuine*—in every sense: natural, original, real, honest, and sincere. (It's 100% you, without 100% of the focus being ON you.)

In another era, we would have simply talked about *reputation*. That worked in a world where certain systems of values predominated, and deviancy from the norm was more likely to be a boat anchor upon your aspirations. Whether as an employee or independent businessperson, a certain degree of homogeneity, at least in regard to certain societal and professional ideals, made sense. There was a common understanding of what constituted a "good reputation."

Today, I smile when I see someone finger-wag someone for dropping a four-letter word in a LinkedIn post. The cussing poster has found a way to run off who they don't want to do business with, and attract those with whom they do. One person's "unprofessional" is the next one's "fun and quirky." And even in cases where "fun and quirky" is a small group against the whole, it might just be a really loyal, super motivated, no limit soldier kind of small group. This is where a *brand* is born. You're one of us. They're not. And we like it that way.

You may feel cheapened and commoditized by talking about your brand, but for some reason it hasn't kept most of us from readily accepting labels of affiliation, perceived quality, and identity, especially among rivals. Urban, suburban, or rural. Blue collar or white collar. Republican or Democrat. Those personal experiences are so strong, that actual corporate brands market to those, and become extensions of them. Can you piece together the profile buyer of the F-150 vs. the Prius brand? I bet you can.

I know. You're unique. Yankees fan. Likes long walks on the beach. A T-shirt and jeans type who still likes getting dressed up to go out on the town. Maybe you're one of the true non-conformists feeling the wind on your face, riding your Harley . . . wearing the same black leather, denim, and metal studs uniform the rest of your fellow non-conformists do. Take that, squares!

Even if somehow you really manage to defy expectations, everyone is still trying to categorize you, anyway. It makes their lives easier. They're not going to stop. So can you see that it might make sense to demonstrate proactively who YOU are, to save them the trouble of deciding for you?

Tribes

A not-really-horrible way of figuring out who you are is simply to figure out who your people are. Whom do you like? Whom do you come from? Who is the most accepting of you? Who has your back?

In other words, whom do you value?

Businesses that think "everyone could be our customer" ride a frantic road to bankruptcy, and people who think everyone is their friend often wind up surprised to find out they don't have any when they need one.

Remember the anecdote about the foul-mouthed LinkedIn post? When you have a flat tire at 2AM, do you want a lot of friendly acquaintances or just one real friend? In this sense, maybe the trend is less towards *personal branding* than it is towards *professional authenticity*. Personally and professionally, we want to focus on what comes naturally and is the most fulfilling. Finding your tribe lets you do that, and having a brand helps your tribe to find you.

But isn't that limiting?

Yes. And like a supply/demand curve should identify an optimal price or a Laffer curve should identify an optimal tax rate, you should recognize there's an optimal point somewhere between a tribe of one (you alone) and 7.7 billion people who find you perfectly agreeable yet somehow avoid ever agreeing to do anything useful for you.

People who say, "I don't care what anyone thinks!" are fools or liars. There is never a third option. We're social creatures. We form a symbiosis with our surroundings. The hermit or off-the-grid mountain man is a myth, and if there were ever a true example of either, it'd be a given that their life would be shorter, harder, and less consequential than it could have been.

If you need a mantra of rugged individualism (which I endorse!), let it be:

"I don't care what *everyone* thinks."

Neutral Colors

If you've ever watched a show on HGTV (Pick one. They're all the same.), then you know you're supposed to paint a house for sale in neutral colors to appeal to the most potential buyers. More prospects, the better chance for an offer. And if there's multiple offers, then you can get a higher price.

But, it might also mean more available substitutes. A 15-year old three bedroom, two-and-a-half bath Colonial in zip code 41507 sells for about the same price as any other approximately 15-year old three-bedroom, two-and-a-half-bath Colonial in zip code 41507. By going with the neutral paint scheme, the real goal is *not* to make yours somehow less appealing than the rest of them to those who are seeking that.

The only way it makes yours worth *more* than the average is if all the others rejected the neutrality advice. Unfortunately for you, everyone else selling a house watched a social worker/poet husband and his teacher/theatre actress wife, earning a joint $72,000, buy a $489,000 house on HGTV, too. They got the "go with neutral colors" memo.

And so it is, too, with all the rote advice on how to get ahead. Dark suit, shined shoes, minimal cologne or perfume, tasteful and limited jewelry, conservative hair, trimmed nails, and a firm handshake. These aren't *bad* things, and they won't hurt you. But this stopped being advice on getting ahead 40 years ago. Now, it's merely a way not to fall behind. I'm not advising against it so much as noting that nobody is special if everybody is. You need more. You need a brand. But, first a cautionary note on. . . .

Literal Branding

Go ahead. Look up "brand." I'll wait. Now, imagine having a literal permanent mark on your rump. Some of you won't have to imagine, because you have one. Maybe not on your rump. Some of you will have it on your shoulder, upper arm, chest, or if you're not confident that those parts won't sag with age and excess carbs, your ankle. Yes, I'm talking about tattoos.

They're not my thing. They never, in my opinion, improve one's aesthetic. Sure, that's judgmental. You didn't get the memo? Judging is a thing, and acting like no one has a right to won't help you.

If there's anything I've heard as often as "I'm not a brand!" it's "My appearance shouldn't matter, only the work that I do!" Again, I get it. You feel like you're being pushed towards something not authentic, and it's a drag. But let me ask, do you *really* only want to be judged by your work. Because, if so, your work must be exceptional and differentiated in every way. Unless you're unquestionably the best at what you do and no one else could compete, I should think you'd be glad to find other selling points about yourself.

You don't care what everyone thinks, and conformity only gets you as far as it gets everyone who conforms. So I'm not telling you not to get a tattoo. Fly your freak flag. Just accept the tribe that's willing to accept you and stop complaining it's not bigger. As I explained, there's a way to optimize your appeal and tribe size. Having these examples of the extremes of being just another replaceable warm body and an entitled egotist, you can better find your balance that is *genuine*, but which attracts *mutual value*.

Be Deliberate

The pushback on the personal branding genre represents a commonly human reaction of "Don't tell me what to do." Thus, what to do and not do is not my focus. Instead, my push on branding is to think about *why* you do what you do, not how to do it. To give you that specific, rote advice isn't merely to make you bland; it's to presume that I know who your target for mutual value is and what is genuine for you. I don't, so I want to help you think about that.

Your brand, as something that optimizes genuineness and mutual value, means that you take a deliberate approach to your external perception instead of a passive one. When you act with purpose, it's strategic. When you do so consistently, it's tactical. Every part of how you present yourself should have thought behind it.

Ever since I was in school, I've used my middle initial. Jared "A." Chambers. Sure, some kids found that funny and likely pretentious. Maybe some adults do now. But I always valued individuality—that's a core value to me. Most everyone uses a first and last name. Including a middle initial is a bit more unique. And while "Jared" isn't the most common name in the world, less so paired with "Chambers," it's bound to be near singular when the middle initial is included. Purpose: "There's only one of me."

Attire is "level-up." I look to denote a level of seniority, which in many circles is synonymous with authority. When you're young, you can achieve this by dressing a little older than your age—stylish, but more classic than trendy. When you're older or among relative peers, you can achieve this by dressing relative to status—business casual over casual, business formal over business casual, etc. I want to be about one level up from the group norm. The objective is differentiation and authority without alienation.

Focusing on the best ways to accentuate yourself isn't pretentious. Too many people look at this in the wrong way. Being the best version of yourself isn't TO NOT be yourself. It's eliminating the static that keeps people from seeing the authentic you, including their own preconceptions, bias, and even simple lack of attention. And there's nothing wrong with turning the volume up or down on certain aspects of your personal presentation as a hook for your audience. Something as mundane as my small talk will not be the same in a group of clinicians as a group of factory workers, though I know from experience that I can authentically, genuinely connect with both.

The next stage is the relationship, which is based on mutual value. Many people have a natural talent for finding their tribe; the rest can be easily taught. Even people who aren't genuine embed themselves in tribes all the time by faking their affinity. I don't suggest it, but it's not hard. Most people are genuinely curious and looking to connect, so the bar can often be pretty low to get in the door. To stay, you have to add value.

Much of my value is around expressing complex ideas in words in a way that connects and persuades. It's not a coincidence that doing so is a part of my brand. I use social media posts, articles, videos, audio recordings, my website, this book, and even correspondence and phone calls to reinforce that crafting messages around the complex, technical, new, controversial, or difficult to explain is what I do. Much of that is fun to me and may not reflect any kind of client work, so it's also very genuine. But I'm also the kind of guy who uses correct punctuation and grammar and a wide vocabulary in text messages. When someone in my tribe thinks about, "Who crafts a really compelling message," I want him or her to think of me.

Personal branding advice that is prescriptive fails because you doing precisely what I do diminishes both our brands—it makes us the same. And we're not really the same, so eventually trying to play someone else's part will look like you forgot all your lines. But if you learn to be deliberate and purposeful, that's a strategy that works for most where you can manage the tactics.

Brand Tactician

Don't worry. I'm not suggesting that now that I've explained *why* that I'm going to leave the *how* entirely up to you. I believe in my ability to sell, that you need to learn more about selling, and that I can bring my ability to your need to boost your professional success. I also recognize some, maybe even you, might already be pretty successful, even more so than I. In fact, I would venture to say it wouldn't be too likely for you to read this book if you didn't already deliver value.

If you could teach me your unique talents, I could combine that with my ability to present the value of those talents to others. In fact, that was my role as a technical salesperson for years. I wasn't an engineer. Or a doctor. Or a software designer. Or a logistics expert. But I could learn enough to speak fluently and intelligently around these topics, and present the information I acquired from true subject matter experts in a way that benefitted the expert and the audience.

Just as I never learned enough to actually BE and engineer, doctor, software designer, logistics expert, etc., I wouldn't expect you to desire or have the ability to sell in the same way that I do. But I can teach you enough to do it sufficiently to use it in combination with your primary expertise to be more valuable.

Helping you think strategically about how to present yourself as a brand is about as good as it gets through a book designed for a mass audience. You'll have to fill in a lot of the gaps yourself with this new framework of how to think about branding. Fortunately, helping you consistently communicate it and present it comprises most of the remainder of this book. Even if you don't perfectly execute upon it, consistently following certain systems will almost certainly differentiate you in a positive way while still very much relying on you to remain centered on who you are and what you do best.

Summing it up

- Your brand has to be genuine, but focused on mutual value of relationships.

- Tribes allow you to be your genuine self, but must be optimized to the reality that you need more than just yourself to exchange in mutual value.

- Deliberately thinking about why you do certain things to connect your genuine self to the opportunity for mutual value is your brand strategy.

- Adopting consistency around communication and selling skills that work in concert with your brand strategy provides you a tactical roadmap that makes you the most compelling as your authentic self.

2 FINANCE & CAPITAL

You probably understand that the point of this "business of one" approach to personal development strategy and better selling yourself is to help you be financially successful. The better you present yourself and strategically orient your talents to others who need them, the more opportunities you'll find to convert that to money. Money is our measure of value, and the economy is the engine by which we can provide direct value to whomever is in need of it, yet obtain that which we need by another who possesses that. It allows us to exchange with anyone we need to without need for direct barter.

But what do you do until you've sold your value? Chicken, meet egg. Egg, chicken. You need money to make money, and the more you have, the more of a force multiplier you have to make even more.

That money to get the ball rolling is capital. You need it. How much will depend on your aspirations. And the strategy—how you sell your value—depends on how much you need later. Those are very personal questions that transcend math. In fact, how most people think about money transcends math. Money is hugely psychological. For example, how people treat plastic money is different from how they treat cash. Math says you'll save more money by paying off a high interest debt first, but psychology says you're more likely to stick to discipline that pays down debts by scoring a fast win by paying off a smaller debt without regard to interest.

As with branding, I respect that you come to the table with some preconceptions. Moreover, in speaking to a general audience, I can't drill into the specifics of your situation. I'm not going to be able to give you a foolproof prescription; I can only give you a systematic framework based in the intuitive reality that you make strategic decisions when you have some breathing room. Without that space, you are more likely to make dumb, desperate choices. That's not strategic. This book is about strategy, so that won't do.

Some will nitpick my strategy, even though I'm not trying to give you a precise roadmap, asserting that they have an unerring formula. Consider that as you decide what makes sense. The self-help genre, like the personal branding genre, is full of folks who think their best appeal to value is to get you to reject all other sources. Their offering is dogma, and they seek to root out the heretics who threaten the sanctity of the message.

You've heard words from them like scarcity, abundance, attraction, laws, consciousness, blah, blah, blah.

None of it means jack if you're broke and can't figure out how to meet your basic needs, much less climb a rung on Maslow's Hierarchy of Needs.

"You can't save your way to wealth!!!"

Bull.

"Growth"-minded folks have this aversion to savings, built on the usual "Let me absurdly polarize common sense so that my message stands out" tactic. They seek to make a binary issue out of a spectrum, which is opposite of my philosophy and first-principle approach. If you're going to find what works for you, "all-or-nothing" may offer appealing promises but is rarely sustainable. I have nothing against growth. I understand that money is as much psychology as math. But people who tell you that you cannot significantly advance your financial position through systematic saving are wrong.

On the argument that "scarcity" thinking harms your ability to grow, perhaps so if it becomes a sole tactic instead of a strategy. That is to say, don't simply be a miser. But not addressing the easiest way to immediately change your financial circumstances—cutting spending—is like thinking you'll be more motivated to get in a workout if you go ahead and order that cheeseburger. The bigger the gap between where you ARE and where you WANT TO BE, the harder it is to get started towards meaningful change.

Not everyone will save as much as I have, and I won't be as rich as some people are. That's okay, and there will always be multiple factors that influence the result. But if you want capital to begin to make different strategic decisions to change your life, especially how you are perceived, you can make an immediate impact by avoiding:

- Eating out.

- Daily morning coffee stop.
- Gym memberships.
- Auto loans and especially auto leases.
- Cable TV.
- Subscription-based services.
- Credit cards.

Again, my approach isn't a list of prescriptive tactics, but rather strategic thinking. If you have a burning desire to do one of these things at some point, even before you become fabulously successful, the world won't have ended. There's such a thing as "wants," and fulfilling certain ones of them, without regard to need. The idea is that you need to be able to distinguish needs from wants, and mindlessly caving to every desire is actually not a motivational program for growth. You won't simply visualize and transformatively create the personal success that fits your outsized lifestyle.

Stop rationalizing something that you want is something that you need:

- I meet potential connections when I go out!
- I'm more productive when I treat myself!
- I need motivation from others to exercise!
- I won't have to worry about repair costs if it's new!
- I work hard so I deserve this.
- If I use this, I'll save money with this plan.
- Airline miles!

If you must do something, categorize it as a want or a need so that you can properly balance the two. But if you lie to yourself that you need ALL of it, you'll find that you always are short of what you need. That's not a "growth mindset." That's poor people acting as if they're rich, and it's the biggest reason they stay poor.

I once heard an overeducated ignoramus offer this justification for taking on a bad client: "Revenue is revenue!"

No, it's not. And revenue isn't the objective, anyway. It's profit. There are a lot of rich people, like big businesses, who manage to move a lot of cash through the year. If all of it goes out as soon as it comes in, or worse, more goes out than in, you simply won't have the flexibility to make different decisions.

"F*** You" Money

You may have heard of the concept of having enough money to say, "F*** you." Somebody asks you to do something you don't want to? "F*** you." You hate your job? "F*** you." Someone tells you no? "F*** you."

Well, understand: there's no sum total that equals "F*** you" money. "F*** you" money is entirely the delta, or net difference, between "What I need" and "What I've got." Get as rich as you want. You'll almost definitely remain poorer than you want on the way there. Yet at any point, the only way you get to say "F*** you" is if you need less than you *already* have. Fortunately, you have control over both. Focusing on one side of the equation to the exclusion of the other is stupid, not some "mindset trick" or "life hack."

Be Deliberate

There it is, again! Being deliberate is probably just a good rule of thumb for everything. Move with purpose. Even if you get a few moves tactically wrong, having the big picture in mind helps to keep you moving strategically, towards your objectives.

Not only do I not offer you a one-size fits all methodology, I don't use one myself. I don't sweat it if I splurge a little on something. I don't keep a written budget. I understand why some people who are starting upside down need a tighter system, more documented, disciplined, and drastic. It's the difference between someone who generally likes eating right and exercising versus someone who's obese in need of a lifestyle intervention. Maintenance is a very different thing from transformation, and when there's not a specific change in state to be attained, the process is its own result.

If you're in need of a financial intervention, there are in-depth resources from experts in turning that situation around. You should work with those people. However, most people manage to pay their bills and keep their lights on and put food on the table. Where they struggle is that after they do those things, there's not much left to invest in their ambitions and not enough that they are free to make big choices without the concern that next month they won't be able to do even basic things. That's a problem when you want to be seen as authentic and valuable—you become reactive and bend in ways you don't want to, just to stay "safe."

The only way to break that cycle, have more freedom, live authentically, and build you unique value is to be deliberate in your relationship with money so that it becomes the propeller of your vision instead of the constant boat anchor. It also lets you get to a place where you're not constantly doing mental math about your bank balance or nervously watching the cash register readout at the grocery store, praying that you didn't exceed your budget.

When you understand the "why" of what you're doing, the "how" is less daunting.

Rules of Thumb

These guidelines keep me on track, and give me a system such that I don't have to spend a lot of time and resources thinking about day-to-day management.

- 1. Default to having more money now.

    Does that sound easy and common sense? Oh, you're already doing that, you say. Then why do you have 96-pack of Dijon mustard from the warehouse club in your pantry. Bulk savings? Probably not, just as a matter of waste, alone. But add up all those little impulse buys that you made *now,* feeling like you'd save money *later,* and it's easy to get in a situation where you don't have emergency funds. That can mean high-interest credit purchases and much less freedom to invest—both real and opportunity costs of the money you tied up to save 48 cents.

    The bulk-pack impulse buy is a funny example. (Because it's true!) But here's another common one, and it's more insidious: Overpaying for a new product and/or warranties to save on repair costs. No one likes feeling like he or she lost. So, having something that's less likely to break, or that will cost less to repair if it does, seems like a smart thing. The math will not bear that out in most cases, though. Instead of paying someone else for this peace of mind, pay yourself. Give yourself the benefit of earning any investment income and interest, and avoid paying inflated costs and interest. When you can choose who holds the money, it should be you that keeps it. Speaking of:

    2. Avoid payments, especially for wants.

    Payments are designed to hide the real cost of something now and make it easier to raise the price of something later. They also keep you in the habit of spending. They let you have new *everything*, but they limit your choices and options. You don't get to say "F*** you" when you're always in hock. Worse, you start to value things that make you less thoughtful and more lazy.

Financing, after all, is not the only kind of payment. Subscription services are, too, and they all make more money when you're as complacent and as unchanging as possible. It's one thing to have a Netflix account (not that you'd die without it), but how many people have Netflix, Amazon Prime, Hulu, cable, a gym membership, a couple online or print periodicals, and some sort of group membership that mostly all go unused while complaining about never having any time? Payments are mostly not strategic, wasteful, and keep you running in place. But,

3. Don't lie to yourself; you're going to spend on wants.

And it's okay. You're better off strategically understanding that you're incapable of giving up all creature comforts and making a plan now than trying to be a monk and giving in to random temptations later.

If you get all hopped up to save money and go cold turkey off leaving the house, entertainment, gifts, and material things, you're going to wind up in a dark place at some point, wondering if it's worth it. It's like a fad diet. Unless you have extreme discipline and internal motivation, you'll reach the intersecting lines on the graph of increasing difficulty and diminishing returns and just give up. Real talk: if you had that kind of motivation, you would never have needed to start on the path of change. Strategy is about thinking ahead and acting when you have control. Figure out what you can live with now and what you can give up, then stick to it. Even so, some things you didn't plan on will come up, so:

4. Have a waiting period on big, non-emergency spending.

People who want your money follow Rule No. 1 religiously—they will always default to having your money now, not later. You should see a theme by now. Those that *have* money and who are good at taking yours are mirror images to each of these rules of thumb. One of their strategies is to create a false sense of urgency and loss aversion by getting you to be reactive with money instead of strategic. Time-based discounts, low-stock, convenient terms—the idea is to get your money now, make you pay the most possible without fully realizing it, and make it easy to keep doing it (or hard to stop).

However, if you understand that money represents value, you'll learn to see through these tricks. Nothing that is a great deal today should not also be a great deal tomorrow. Sleep on it. Even if it's gone tomorrow, it will be back again. You'll find the great deals if you:

5. Put time on your side.

Even for things you need, there's no need to be in dire need before you look around. Emergencies happen, but even many of those can be mitigated. Thinking ahead will let you walk away from more bad deals and give you appropriate breathing room to sleep on it.

I will always be in the market for certain things. Clothing. Food. Maintenance items for the home or the car. At first, this may seem to conflict with Rule No. 1. In fact, this rule of thumb is one that will still require a bit of daily judgment and discernment without being completely on autopilot. You have to manage your own inventory and have experiential knowledge of when things run out or die. If the battery in my truck is five years old, knowing that they mostly have a 3-5 year lifespan, I'd rather start looking for sales on new ones than pay the time cost of being eventually stranded, have limited options of worse deals, and pay for extras like an Uber ride or a tow. Thus, Rule 5 is in concert with Rule 1. The time value of money is about optimizing both, so you get the most value out of your money.

These five rules of thumb will give you a fine maintenance program that will enhance your power if you've already achieved a degree of financial self-sufficiency. If you're just starting out, they will create the foundation for achieving it. If you've made some big mistakes, you may well need more structure and tactical methods than this to right your financial ship, for which there are many resources. I'm not offering exhaustive financial advice, but rather helping you demonstrate high value by giving you stability in the metric by which we measure and exchange value—money.

Summing it up

- Money is how we measure value, and a tool to build your vision, as capital. Selling your value will always be tied to how you handle it.

PROFESSIONAL PERCEPTION

- Making money is the objective, but saving it is the fastest short-term path to changing your circumstances and having options.

- It's okay to want things, but don't rationalize them as something you need. Categorize so that you prioritize.

- The greater what you have right now is compared to what you immediately need, the more options you will have.

- If you use purposeful strategy, you won't have to pore over every decision with money. First principles will guide you, and you will demonstrate value in your stability and power of choice.

3 NEGOTIATION

You know who you are (brand) and what you've got (finance). Really, we just now get to the point of it all: If you want who you are and what you've got to mean enough to anyone else so that you don't end up being something else and having nothing, you have to negotiate with others.

Of course, as with much of what we've already covered, the word alone probably gives you a bit of heartburn. For many, "negotiate" has a negative connotation. Logical—same root! From the Latin, *negotium*. "*Neg*" as in "not." "*Otium*" meaning "leisure." Literally, "not leisure." That means it's business! So we might as well get down to it.

Your experience negotiating probably centers around things like buying cars, where someone is trying to get as much of your money as possible, or discussing salary at a job, where someone is trying to give you as little money as possible. Neither experience leaves you with the warm fuzzies. And if you leave negotiating to this default status, that's all it will ever be—two sides trying to extract the most for themselves from what appears as a fixed value. Zero-sum negotiating occasionally results in what seems like a fairly even splitting of the difference—fair, but not really a win. Mostly, one side has to lose for the other to win. It's more about taking value than exchanging it, and it's certainly not about creating it.

I'm going to teach you to teach you to see this in a new way. Why? Well, that paradigm shift to maximizing your value using a business-oriented framework is sort of the point of this book! Truly, this is the one foundational skill to everything else. Personal branding and finance just give you a way to define roles and understand the stakes. Negotiation is a system unto itself, and it will connect you to the world in a closed loop. Your understanding of it will inform the principles by which you interact with the world.

As with all the skills I cover here, I use a business perspective for consistency—establishing a new system by which you increase your perceived value. As a career salesperson and manager, my experience with negotiation in business is deep. However, I also enhanced my natural aptitude in negotiation through a training and licensing to become a civil mediator. I'm going to save you several grand and a couple weeks of your time with this major spoiler from mediation training. It should guide every future negotiation of which you are a part: What people tell you they want is almost never the actual reason they're beating the hell out of you to get whatever that thing is. They may be honest about what they want, but they often mislead about why they want it. Learn to take things to a more fundamental level, and you'll find more ways for both sides to win through creating value.

Oh, yeah. Now's a good time to dig into this "perceived value" concept. We've discussed value already, in terms of mutual value and measuring value. But it's worth noting that as much as we try to objectify the concept, it's always subjective. Everyone gets to decide what's valuable *to him or her*. Sure, there are some similarities between people that increase to likelihood that any rando on the street will value certain basic things. Fulfill basic biological needs; that's valuable. Help others do functions that they go about in meeting their own daily needs; also valuable. But, and like a Kardashian sister, this is a big ol' but: The things that are the most *universally valuable* are also the *least differentiated*. Substitutes are myriad.

All of us—this is the universal, hard-wired part that is part of being human—make predictions about the future when we ascertain our perception of value. Even if we are meeting a basic biological need, it is to ensure we persist into the future. You're evolutionarily designed to live as long as possible, then pass on your genes to a new generation. Also, we naturally communicate, working to pass on our ideas and the products of our knowledge. Our decisions are future-based, even if only the near-term future. If I'm hungry, and I choose something to eat, it's with the expectation that I won't be hungry *after* I eat. What you do *now* always is tied to the result *after*.

But there's a catch. We're really bad at predicting things. Many of the things evolution designed us to do by default are the things we also recognize as huge flaws. Stereotypes, biases, logical fallacies—these are little more than pattern-matching algorithms to help us figure out what will likely result from a given action or circumstance. But just as we design computer algorithms around the idea of "fail-to-safe," nature didn't make us to be perfect. What it did is to make it such that failures in our judgment aren't catastrophic. For example, poison ivy has leaves in clusters of three. If I avoid every three-leaved plant in the woods, they may not all be poison ivy. In fact, none may be. I might be wrong a thousand times to one treating the plants I've encountered as if they're all poison ivy. But if I stick to the logic, however flawed, I will never touch real poison ivy, either. I also don't waste useful time fretting over botanical identification. Little to lose and a lot to win.

In ascertaining value, our perception is every bit as a) future-oriented, b) systematically consistent, and yet c) logically flawed. That's what this whole book is about. There are some human consistencies in how our perceptions are formed, yet we still come up with unique perceptions. You can us the commonality in how we form perceptions to help you align others' perceptions to yours or predict who might be inclined to perceive things as you do. That's why the techniques described in this book are strategic, but leave flexibility on tactics.

The most useful concept of value perception that I found in 20 years of selling and a lifetime as a student of how people communicate is that perceived value is a ratio of Upside potential to Downside potential. In other words, *we perceive value as a degree of risk.*

Something with little downside and high upside is an easy choice. High downside and little upside, we'll avoid that option. You can pinpoint most any self-calculated ratio in decision making along an *x-y* axis I call a "Risk Perception Value Matrix."

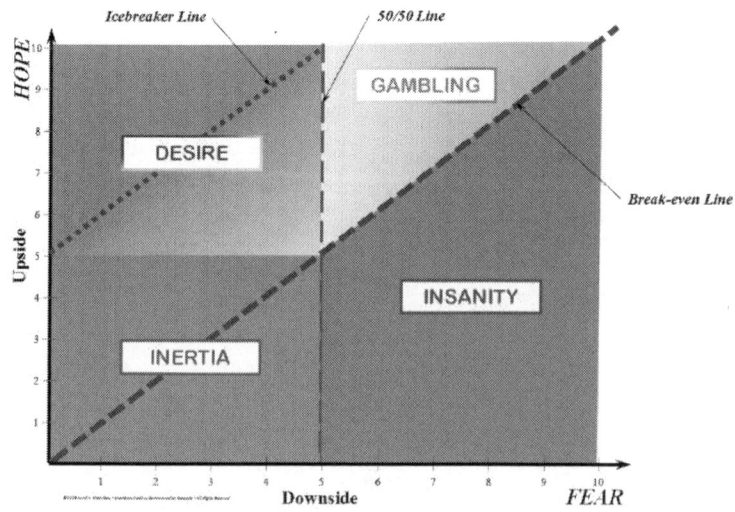

RISK PERCEPTION VALUE MATRIX

Don't bog down in the details too much for now. The quadrants mostly emphasize someone's probability in making an affirmative choice based on how they view the potential. It's a way to try to visualize general mindset as people compare what good might come from a choice versus what bad might happen, and it's worth noting that most people overemphasize the bad in the first place. (Back to the fail-to-safe idea—loss aversion guides our thinking.) In that sense, even Upside and Downside, as fiscal-based terms of risk, are imprecise. If you prefer, think of it as a ratio of hope to fear. The more hope outweighs fear, the higher value we place on a thing.

In negotiating and selling, most people hammer on the hope side. It's natural to keep focusing on the expected good thing that happens if someone will only do what we are asking. More money, more friends, more sex, more life, MORE! You've probably lived long enough to know the limits of that approach. If it worked, no one would ever say no to anything. They might agree with the positives, but will still see it as a gamble if you've not addressed their fears. Some cynical negotiators, noting that limitation, hammer only on fear. You're going to lose everything if you don't do this one thing! That moves some people that hope didn't work on, but there's still a wide gap. If the choice you present allays those fears but offers little other potential to hope for, the choice can get bogged in inertia, paralyzing any change in course.

It's helpful to understand there's a difference between someone agreeing with you and you having convinced them. Highlighting upside or downside exclusively helps you connect with the agreeable, who, with your gentle reminder, already share your understanding of what is positive or negative. But it's not a skill aligned with convincing somebody who's not inclined to go along, which is where negotiation begins.

To be an effective negotiator, you have to have a holistic view of both upside and downside, and be able to understand how those play to another person's hopes and fears. You have to take an intangible view of tangible things, working on a conceptual level. As an example, let's use money to represent the tangible. As such, upside and downside may represent a typical fiscal viewpoint of profit and loss, a tangible, objective thing.

Many people negotiate to the universal and the tangible. Most people would rather have more money than less of it. This should make every sale, every negotiation, every conflict resolution an easy thing. Instead, there are a great many lost opportunities, stalemates, and irreconcilable differences.

Beyond value, money might represent to someone:

- Prestige

- Achievement
- Safety
- Freedom
- Connection to religious or moral values

These will motivate people in different ways, each factor weighted towards one's experiences, culture, education, relationships, and beliefs.

If you're going to be a great negotiator, you need to:

- Make better than average predictions of outcomes based on given circumstances, adjusting the probabilities of multiple outcomes as the circumstances evolve.
- Communicate those results and likely ramifications in a convincing way.
- See a person's motivations at a more fundamental level than the tangible.
- Find common connections between the result you want and what someone else wants, and show how circumstances can be adjusted to provide an optimal outcome.

It's an art form that you will never perfect. But the more you practice, the better you will get and the more indispensible others will perceive you to be.

People and Energy

As noted, people are bad at predicting the future. Yes, that includes you. I've had a few wins that I'm proud of, but also more misses than I can count. Most people think that the way to improve is to outsmart their hard wiring, which as we discussed, gets everyday predictions wrong in favor of being right in a life or death scenario. It just doesn't work to try to outsmart your own evolution. Even if you were perfectly logical and capable of getting outside of your own head to evaluate people objectively, it wouldn't help you. Your fellow man still will be subjective, flighty, and illogical.

While it's good to improve your logic and reason to examine non-human factors, know your limits when people are inevitably reintroduced as a variable to your balanced equation. I can tell you that I have good instincts about people, and those gut feelings rarely steer me wrong. If anything, I am more often wrong because I disregarded a feeling that I couldn't logically explain to someone else. I don't know if my instincts are better or worse than yours, because we have no objective way to measure. I only know what's normal to me. The most objective way for me to explain to you how to hone your instincts is try to read people's energy.

On value perception, I described it as the ratio of hopes to fears. Think of hope as positive and fear as negative. (Not in a judgmental sense—people's motivations are valid to them, and that's all that matters.) These are like opposing forces found in nature, like magnetism, electricity, etc. A starting point can be as simple as whether you feel positive or negative energy from a person:

Positive Energy	Negative Energy
• Open gestures / stance	• Closed body language
• Communicative	• Insular
• Inquisitive / curious	• Uninterested
• Knowledge-seeking	• Validation-seeking
• Content, excited, happy, or similar emotions	• Gruff, irritable, or similar emotions

Let me again reiterate that this is not a judgment of right or wrong of motivation or personality. One can emote positive energy angling for advantage. One might emote negative energy seeking to protect and defend vital interests. Think of these as energy states like electrical wires—both are necessary.

But this initial read of a person is a starting point to knowing whether they might be more receptive to an upside case or a downside one. And ultimately, I never use one to the exclusion of the other. Negotiating is a process of alignment, which requires calibration. Understanding initial state, you will continually measure for feedback and changes along the way.

The Power of Questions

Don't worry. You're not just trusting your intuitive read on energy. Your most powerful tool in negotiating is asking questions, true for two reasons:

- Questions discover useful information. (Duh!)
- Questions let you present ideas without raising objection.

A negotiation isn't over until there are no more questions. You want that to be at the point that the answer to the final question is "yes." Along the way, the answer to many will be "no." If you don't know how to ask a question that extracts new info to let you go forward a different way or a question that plants an idea that persuades a reconsideration, your negotiation will end with your last question being the final question, and the answer being "no." That is a bad thing, unless you agree that the "no" actually means that there's no opportunity to exchange mutual value in a way in which both sides remain genuine to who they are. (That happens, and it's why we covered those concepts first.)

At the beginning of any negotiation, I want the other side talking as much as possible. Anything I say has the potential to go down an unintended rabbit-hole, and it won't be tailored to the concerns and relevance of the other side. I don't do pitches, demos, opening statements, blind presentations or proposals, or anything of the like without first letting the other side talk and asking them questions.

That accomplishes many things. Others are more engaged and less defensive when you're talking if they feel that they've been heard. But more than that, I actually listen. Gauge emotions. Look for discrepancies between what they claim to want and their attachment to or investment in a single outcome. See how well they understand their own position. Do they try to obscure their own lack of understanding about a situation? The more they see me trying to understand, the more I take on a role of trust as an advisor, mediator, business resource, or even just an adversary, but one who comes in good faith seeking a fair solution.

When it is time for me to talk, it can then be laser-focused on both their stated concerns, and more importantly, their unstated actual ones. I am then answering their questions, and that has power over people. Give them answers to what they want to know, and you will build a relationship. It earns you the right to ask the final question in a negotiation, and have them willingly answer "yes." When's the last time someone answered every question you had in a reassuring way, and you still said, "No?" I rest my case.

The Funnel

In sales, the process is often described as a funnel. That process is a negotiation, broader on one end because new opportunities must enter at a higher volume to maintain a consistent flow of sales coming out. But it's also helpful to look at the inflow as broader than the outflow because the beginning is where you ask the broadest questions based in the *now* and narrower at the far side because that is where you will ask tightly-focused questions that affect future state.

I don't argue that it's a perfect model, but it does help define a consistent process that gives you a first-principles-based system.

The opening of your funnel should have open-ended questions. There's no need to plant statements in the form of a question. *"What do you think about x?" "What do you want me to know?" "What should I understand about this?"* A natural follow-up is the ubiquitous, *"Tell me more..."*

You are finding out about the present state, aligning your negotiation in the present. Timing is everything! Move too far in the future with the negotiation process OR what might happen in the future, and you will lose people. As you move forward in the funnel, you will be exploring potential by asking more focused, targeted questions about specifics of the situation. *"What happens because of x that you mentioned?" "What would you like to see happen?" "How will you be affected if things stay the same?"* And as you move into the narrowest end, you can help them envision the outcomes of different futures in terms of guiding them towards where you can address the upside and the downside in a way that fits their comfort with risk. *"Have you considered the possibility of x?" "I understand x that you said, but what if y?""How would you feel about x result?"*

Right energy. Right questions. Right time-alignment. Every situation is different, but if you practice towards mastering these, your negotiations will evolve into not just acceptable results, but effective relationships.

No

Much of the preceding assumes you in the role of the negotiation initiator. In some negotiations, one side takes a more active role and the other more passive. In others, it will be roughly equal. Everything offered so far in this chapter is useful from either side. From an active or passive perspective, but especially the passive, the word "no" is a powerful tool.

"No" resets everything. You want something from me that I don't think is fair? "No" is a red flag that we are out of alignment, and you have to better establish the value to me or change what you're asking. I've made you an offer and you don't think it's fair? "No" lets you maintain your value and test perceptions.

I've used "No" from a buyer's and a seller's perspective in my work and life. Many people make the mistake of readily using it as a buyer, but not a seller. Why not? Do you want to give your value away to a parasite that was running a reverse sell on you, trying to convince you that your offer was unfair? You almost always can rescind a no if you later decide it doesn't make sense. As I said, it's mostly a reset point, and barring being simply too far apart, negotiation resumes. And if you're just too far apart, think of the time savings!

No is also very powerful in conflict resolution negotiations. If you make someone a fair offer in response to a stated demand from the other side, and they tell you no, you have more digging to do on the root problem. If someone makes you an offer based on positional dynamics (I started here, and you started there, so let's just meet in the middle.) without attempting to answer your true problem, telling them no forces them to listen, not merely bargain.

"No" is hard for some people because of that risk thing, again. See, the Risk Perception Value Matrix isn't just describing *other* people. It's describing *all* people. That means you. You're going into a negotiation with a look at your upside and downside, too, manifested as what you hope and fear. Some salespeople never say "no" because the fear of losing the sale weighs more heavily than the hope of a more profitable sale. Some people won't say no in a conflict resolution because their fear of looking foolish for their motivations or having an escalation outweighs the hope of getting an outcome they actually consider fair.

This means it is crucial to walk into every negotiation—buying, selling, interviewing, reviewing, mediating, litigating, etc.—as prepared as possible on both the objective merits of the situation (financial, legal, what have you) and the subjective (your criteria of what you can live with.) Know the situation, know yourself, and know what you're willing to walk away from. But, how do you know that?

Be Deliberate

Unless you're skipping around the book (Stop that! Commit to the process!), you should be sensing a pattern here. I've said yes to a great many things I regret. I cannot seriously recall anything to which I regret saying no. Why? It goes back again to the order in which I've covered things. I know who I am. I understand how to measure value. When you are squared away on who you are as a person, who your tribe is, what your financial needs are, and your system for meeting them, you simply kick to the curb anything that significantly disrupts those principles and systems.

The beauty of first-principle thinking is that not every decision is overwhelming. You have the basic building blocks. You get to be cool while someone else is scrambling. YOU are actually learning to get in touch with the future, because you're being strategic. Nature may have shorted us on the ability to predict outcomes, but the next best thing is to create an outcome, by default, because no one else thought ahead that far.

Based on your desire to improve by reading this book, you likely have read other books in subjects such as manifesting your thoughts, law of attraction, and creating things from your thoughts. I have. I'm not sold on the metaphysical side. (Although, I don't entirely discount it, either.) But enough successful people have used those systems that they intrigue me and demonstrate at least some merit. Logically, what I can say is that if you can sell to or negotiate with others, it reasons that you can do so with yourself. Specifically, how far can you get in convincing someone else if you *haven't* convinced yourself? If you're consistently deliberate, consistently strategic, consistently thinking about your genuine self and mutual value, you default to things that reinforce that reality and shun those that don't. You simply say no to future outcomes you don't want, and that has a strong influence on getting ones that you do.

Maybe that's a secret. It's some sort of divine providence, or that you learned to program the code of the universe, or something else requiring the strong smell of incense to ponder fully. But it could be just an everyday miracle like waking up and breathing—do what comes naturally and be good, or practice and be amazing. Who's to say which is more inspired?

Summing it up

- Negotiation is the exchange of value, and people perceive value as a ratio of risk of what they hope to gain versus what they fear losing.

- Decision-making is future-oriented, though people are not good at predicting all possible outcomes. They are mostly wired to avoid bad ones.

- Find someone's flow of energy to get an initial read on whether they are more likely to be influenced by gain or loss, but always address both. Move their perception to where upside outweighs downside.

- Align the negotiation process as a funnel. Ask broad questions around the past and present, moving to narrow questions that focus on the future.

- Reset the negotiation process at any time by either party saying "no" and being willing to walk.

- Know your boundaries by having confidence in the process as well as your understanding of self, value, and needs. Create the desired outcome by accepting only the desired outcome.

4 WRITING

For starters, you're not very good. Believing that you are, or that there's not much of a difference between a good writer and a bad one other than how well they know grammar and spelling, gets in your way. Grammar and spelling aren't to be dismissed, but I'll let you in on a secret: Some great writers struggle with those things, and some atrocious writers have advanced language arts degrees.

Of course, as I have from the beginning, I speak in generalities for a broad audience. You may be the exception, a great writer. Most are not. And even if you feel that you are, I hope you'll consider that not all "great writing" suits all purposes. Being a great house painter doesn't make you Picasso, nor do we have evidence that Picasso was someone you'd hire to paint houses. Writing is such a craft. Some carpenters build homes, others make fine furniture. Both are carpenters. Either may display aptitude to cross over into the other niche. Many people intuitively understand the difference. For whatever reason, this understanding doesn't translate to writing. Consider:

- People hire out-of-work journalism majors to write their résumés.

- Technical writers often have English degrees but no technical background.

- Business owners write their own marketing copy.

- Proposals are largely written by technical experts who have no professional writing experience, then edited by "proposal writers" who have no technical familiarity.

Do you still doubt me that most folks are bad writers? Okay. How much writing do you see that is good? If you've screened employees, do you find most resumes to be so good that you find it difficult not to interview everyone? Are instructions that come with the things you buy helpful, or do you toss them aside or try to use them and become frustrated? Are you rushing out to buy things from every promotional flyer in the mail you receive? Have you ever read a sales proposal from cover to cover without simply looking at the last page for the price, then only skimming and searching the rest if you had an unanswered question? I think you get the idea.

I'm sure you're ready for the good news! Sorry. I haven't even gotten to the bad news yet. The bad news is that this one chapter in this one book can't make you a good writer. It also can't make you a writer for all genres. If you really want to improve, it's going to take a lot of practice, and I don't mean long-winded blog and social media posts that your friends read but others find cringe-inducing.

I'm sorry for the dim view, but I need to ground you in reality so that you can appreciate the good news. Ready? *When most writing sucks, you don't need to be good to stand out. You simply need to be better.*

There's a one-degree difference between really hot water and boiling water. Sometimes it's the marginal that makes a profound difference. This is one of those times. You can read, study, and practice specialized writing if you have a desire to become a good writer, and for projects outside your skill or scope, you probably should just hire a writer. It is a profession, you know! There's no shame in it not being your profession. Being able to perform first aid doesn't make you a doctor, but not being a doctor shouldn't keep you from knowing basic first-aid. That's what I'm offering you—writing first-aid. Let's stop the bleeding!

First Principles

At the very least, understand what good writing is and what good writers do to become good. If you do that, it's hard not to become better if you consistently put it to practice. Let's tackle these one by one.

Writing Is a Means, Not an End

Too often, we talk about writing as a work product—something we create or pay for. As such, people overanalyze it as a piece of work. Should I have used this word instead of that word? Did I say everything I wanted to say? Did I pick the right font? People fall in love with the words on the page and forget the point they intended to make. Do you know how many hours I've spent on professional writing projects having non-writers critique every. Single. Word. Choice? You can't call yourself a professional writer if you've not had someone argue with you about whether to use "often" or "frequently."

The point of writing is to get the audience to understand something *as you understand it*. You are conveying an idea, thought, or intended action. Good writing helps your audience share the idea, thought, or follow through on the intended action that *you* have in mind. Shared language, and the consistently correct use of it, provides a common reference to communicate the thought as clearly as possible. But if you're pedantically combing over the subtleties of definitions or judging the result by whether all the sentences diagram nicely, you're not focusing on whether the reader has a common understanding with the writer. Good writers care about whether the reader understands. Amateur writers fuss over word choices and obscure rules because they have little other value to add.

Read

I've seen myriad online writing challenges, such as those suggesting you write for a set duration of time each day for a set period, such as 30 days. Practice, practice, practice! Practice makes perfect!

No.

Perfect practice makes perfect. You've probably heard athletes say this. Perhaps it's oversimplified, but the point is if you do something incorrectly, doing it often won't help you to improve. If anything, it reinforces incorrect form. You must have an objective standard against which to measure progress and constant feedback to conform to that standard. The *only* way to do that is by reading. Read for depth and understanding. Read the kinds of things you wish to write. Think about the things that helped you understand something for the first time, or which changed an understanding you previously held.

The more you read, the more you intuitively understand spelling, sentence structure, grammar, and even style. That beats all of the classroom teaching in the world. You'll imitate what you see. And the more you read from different places, the more that imitation will synthesize into your own unique voice and style of writing that captures the best elements of what you read. Read, *then* write. Only then will further practice help.

If Your Writing Depends On Being Read, You've Failed

What? You thought you were the only one not reading? You're not alone. It's time consuming and most writing lacks the relevance and clarity that makes it worth the time to try to process it. As an editor, I don't know how many times I've heard pleas of, "But I need to add in this, or the audience won't understand!" My answer is always the same, "You can edit this down with purpose, or your reader will decide what to edit out later. If this makes or breaks things, you need to start over."

The impulse of most people is to "information dump." Meaning, they want to say everything in their mind and anticipate every question, and drop it in front of the audience. That's poor writing, and is the written equivalent of a stranger latching on to you and telling you their life story as you try politely to get away. Just as everything else I cover in this book, writing is about engaging with others productively, and it's always a process.

Your best tool is brevity. The less there is to read, the less objection there is to reading. People also read in predictable ways to try to discern the point quickly. Beginning and end—that's what people read. The middle is filler. That's true on a document level or a paragraph level. Put the important stuff FIRST and LAST. That's an *and*, not an *or*. If it's important, state it more than once. And no, don't go out of your way to say it differently so that it's not redundant. You're reinforcing a point, so don't hide it. While we're on this idea . . .

Junior Year Composition Was Wrong

You remember, don't you? Bigger words. More words. Don't use the same word twice. Don't split your infinitives. Don't end a sentence with a preposition. Am I stirring your memory of red ink and some fussy Brunhilda lecturing you?

Well forget it.

Grammar and style are important. But think of high school composition class as a boot camp. The point is to drill you and develop consistent patterns. They make you sound more "adult." They give you an understanding of language. Boot camp, but not combat training. You're not ready for real world writing that actually achieves something other than a letter grade until you know how to take that basic training and improvise in the real world.

So not only are you looking for simpler words and fewer words. Not only are you intentionally using repetition to make a point. You will also learn that grammar "rules" are idealized suggestions. If they were immutable, language would never change. And in fact, some of the "rules" always had exceptions. Those who tell you that you can never end a sentence with a preposition? Pedantic *and* factually wrong! In general, given the choice between strict adherence to a rule and being clear, choose clear.

Practical Skills

Using first principles, you can develop some basic skills and practices that will make your writing stand out. They may not make you a writer, and that's okay. Who wants to be something they're not? I'm not a lot of the things in which I have basic skills that allow me to a) do-it-myself on small projects, and b) recognize quality craftsmanship. This allows me to either do-it-myself competently to save money, or make a more informed decision when obtaining professional help. Confucius say, "Man who can do own laundry not get taken to cleaners!"

Let us first distill the four first principles into simple rules of thumb:

1. Maintain clarity through purpose.

2. Put into practice the best of what you've read.

3. Be brief, but anything important is worth saying twice.

4. Rules are for the guidance of the wise and the obedience of fools.

There are some basic forms of writing that are like changing a tire or fixing a dripping faucet. You don't have to be a "writer" any more than you need to be a mechanic or a plumber. The basic skills are good for your wallet and potentially save you from a jam.

The premise of this book is that you can better sell yourself and achieve what most of us recognize as success by thinking of yourself as a business—the CEO of Self, Inc. As such, there's no more ubiquitously useful piece of writing as the business letter.

Business Letters - Writing Yourself Blank Checks

The basic structure of a business letter can be repurposed for many specific pieces of writing:

- Cover letters for employment

- Informal sales proposals and price quotations

- Grievances

- Thank you and follow-up letters

- Requests for in-person meetings

- Responses to any of the above correspondence

It's impossible to tally precisely the dollars I've put in my pocket directly related to letter writing, but it's a lot. In fact, taken to this basic level of employment and earning sales, probably *every* dollar I've ever earned is tied to letter writing. Moreover, I've recouped at least tens of thousands for myself and companies I've worked for in refunds, rebates, and other remediation for specific grievances. Good business letters are as good as checks—blank checks—that you write and which the other party fills in the amount. That's power. It may represent the most direct Return On Investment (ROI) that you'll get from this book. In fact, it's one of the few areas of this book that I switch from strategy to tactics. Business letters done well are that powerful, and a scripted formula makes it nearly impossible to fail if you use it consistently from first principles.

AIDA

"*AIDA. Attention! Interest! Decision! Action! Attention. Do I have your attention? Interest. Are you interested? I know you are, 'cause it's f*** or walk. You close or you hit the bricks. Decision. Have you made your decision for Christ? And action. AIDA. Get out there. You got the prospects coming in; you think they came in to get out of the rain? A guy don't walk on the lot lest he wants to buy. They're sitting out there waiting to give you their money. Are you going to take it? Are you man enough to take it?*" — "Blake" in *Glengarry Glen Ross*

The above quote from a scene of salesman lore is perhaps oversimplified. If you've seen the movie, you may think the concept is pure fiction. But, A-I-D-A is a long-used marketing format, and we can expand on the basics that Blake succinctly laid out.

AIDA is a four-part format that quickly aligns the reader to a negotiation cycle. (I told you to read the book in order! Go back to Chapter 3 if you must!) It's emotional and logical. It's necessarily brief. It's audience-centric without leaving the end hanging with them in control of the cycle.

Attention: Because people don't read, your best chance is to hook them right from the start. A letter's open shouldn't be small talk, apologies for taking the reader's time, or thanking them for reading. (Premature with such a lousy hook!) You must be direct to the point with the subject, but in the reader's frame of reference. The easiest hook is an insightful question that is important to your audience. Or, establish a framing that shows you understand an issue or topic from their point of view. One way to do that is offer a unique piece of information appealing to their perspective that they may not have realized. (As long as you can quickly and credibly back it up, a jarring statistic of which they're likely to be skeptical is a good approach.) Also, you can juxtapose them to an idealized version of self or a competitor in some respect. The idea with all three approaches is that their mind engages in terms of a response. Of course, you're writing, so they can't immediately respond. So they read on:

Interest: You have their attention, so interest them! This is harder than it sounds. The natural impulse many writers have after they've captured someone's attention is to pelt them with facts, anecdotes, features, and benefits of a proposal. These are not interesting. Seriously, are you interested when people start talking *at you* with no clue *about you*? If you are, let's exchange contact info so you can accompany me to functions and stand in when people start doing this to me.

No, what's interesting to most people is *them*. Tell them about themselves. Maybe something you've learned about them or more about a problem you've anticipated that they have. You are not, as a matter of interest, going to talk at all about *you* yet. And if you're keeping score, that's two defined sections where you or anything about you is not part of the program.

Decision: (Alternately called "Desire" in some marketing texts.) Before others can do whatever it is you want, they have to have reinforcing information to make a choice. Bear in mind, "do nothing" is the default choice, so your Attention hook better still be in play and the Interest that you built should be real and relevant to the audience. They have to *want* to do what it is you need them to do.

Now you can talk about you. But not all of you, please. You have to close the loop on the connection you're building from Attention and Interest to the intended Action only. For example, if you're writing to score an interview with a cover letter, DON'T close on why to hire you. It's out of timing and out of cycle. Think about *why* someone interviews multiple candidates instead of hiring the first qualified warm body coming in the door—risk! Risk of making a poor choice. Risk of not getting the most they can. Make yourself a low-downside consideration. Differentiate yourself vis-à-vis this stage of the decision process and no more. (Clarity. Purpose. Brevity.)

Action: By now, the next step should feel natural and good to your audience. They will make a choice. But if you've done everything right, it won't entirely be up to them. You must ask them to do whatever it is you need them to do. And you have to make it easy. Things that are not easy reintroduce risk to the scenario. So it can't be simply, "Well, call me!" or "Hope to chat soon!" or "Could we meet sometime?" Anything open-ended forces them to make a complicated choice of opportunity cost and investment of time. Still, I'm honestly not a fan of the, "I will call you Tuesday at 10 unless I hear otherwise" approach. You didn't take away a complicated choice—now they have to decide where to be to avoid your pushy self come mid-morning Tuesday.

People freeze up with unbounded choices, but bristle against feeling as if they have no choice. Offer up several options that are all a win for you. I don't like either/or. Three is perfect. (I will reserve either/or for the context of a hardball negotiation, but that's why I otherwise opt for three. It feels less like a hardball negotiation.) An idealized choice that seems like it's off the table is powerful, too. "I understand you may need some time to arrange a formal meeting in with your team, but I'm available to talk by phone Tuesday morning or just to stop by and introduce myself when I'm in the area Thursday." Questioning one's readiness to accede to your most desirable option tends to make them consider it. But any next step you've offered is a win.

Formatting

AIDA is a structural formal to link how you write to how you negotiate. So whether you're writing letters, proposals, marketing copy, or just telling a story in writing, you're obligated to write according to first-principles. Every strategy I outline in this book builds on the previous one, and sticking to systems that develop from those ideas will put you ahead of the curve.

Still, writing is a complexity that you won't master immediately. In the near-term, there is one thing you can do above all others that will set you above 98% (okay, I made that up, but close) of your competition: Format the layout of your documents correctly. There are too many books and too many templates as demonstration for you to wing it. Yet, most people do. Common documents like business letters, résumés, memos, etc. that look like you just opened a blank document in Word, started typing, and just used the space bar and hard returns for layout get trashed. Your writing will improve over time from following the principles I've provided. You'll get the chance to improve simply by using available tools to make your writing *look* like the product of a professional. Being perceived as professional . . . Wow! Is there a theme here, or what?!

Be Deliberate

First principles and AIDA will get you through much of your day-to-day, objective-oriented writing. Closing the loop on both, it's worth reiterating this theme of deliberation. Know your objective when you start writing. Write. Edit out every word that doesn't support the objective. Even professional writers churn out unreadable garbage because they apply their skills in genre of writing, such as journalism or English composition, to the wrong context, such as sales copy or technical manuals. Or, simply because they are cowards that won't push back against managers, marketers, and tech wizards who fall in love with their own BS, they produce poor copy that doesn't reflect their skill.

I've fought these battles for twenty years in business, getting people to write for what their audience needs to hear rather than what they want to say. I've deleted dozen-paged "Executive Summaries" and "Introductions" that said nothing about the audience or their concerns. Such masturbatory marketing prose bragging about self and company are the first things I eliminate, only to have someone try to sneak it back in the final copy.

Know your audience. Know your objective. Know what ties those together. Write that. Delete words that aren't that. Put it in a clean, readable document of correct layout. There. You can now write virtually anything you'll ever need to get what you want, better than almost anyone.

Summing It Up

- Even most "professional" writing is bad, so consistently applying a few basic principles and skills will set you apart in achievement.

- The product of writing isn't the words on the page, but achieving your purpose in writing them. Maintain clarity towards that.

- Read the kind of writing that you want to do, and incorporate what works into your own.

- People avoid deep reading, so keep it short and emphasize key points, even if seemingly redundant.

- Rules are for the guidance of the wise and the adherence of fools. Do not ever sacrifice clarity for the sake of an obscure "rule."

- In terms of practical writing, business letters serve most of your purposes. Apply first principles, AIDA format, and proper layout.

- You're writing for the audience, not yourself. Know what matters to them and to you. Link those things. Get rid of everything else.

5 PRESENTATION & SPEAKING

If there's a skill that the average person will at eventually be called on to do in a professional setting that they do less well than writing, it's public speaking. You may have been asked to do a presentation at some point and did not enjoy it. That's okay, because your audience was miserable, too. In fact, if you'd noticed that the audience was still there, in the room, while you were somewhere in your own head trying not to forget this one thing that's super important, you'd have realized they were zoned out and not listening, anyway.

The principles of good writing and good presentations or speaking are not so different. Re-read the last chapter, replacing the word "writing" with "speaking" and "reading" with "listening," and you'll be on your way to better presentations.

However, a key difference is that you actually have to face your audience. That's the hang-up most people have. You have to be the person that bores everyone, or is too obtuse to know they're boring, or the arrogant lecturer, or the timid newbie that some heckler tears into. Frankly, I think the reason most people hate speaking and presenting is the same one that justified public hangings as a crime-deterrent. No one watches and thinks, "Man, I'd like to be up there someday!"

Of course, like public hanging, this all leaves one wondering why something that many find callous, undignified, and even cruel hasn't also rendered public speaking a relic. Maybe it's because, for all the pain, some presenters manage to delight us, being both entertaining and informative. Or, we're sadists. For my purposes, I will assume the former and try to help you be more delightful, entertaining, and informative.

Where Speakers Fail

In addition to applying the first principles and practical skills of writing to your presentations, the next best "hack" is simply to avoid the most common pitfalls of presentations that drive you nuts and make you want to run far, far away. We've all been there, so let's catalogue the top offenses:

- **Doing an unnecessary presentation:** From company meetings that could have been a memo to first-visit sales calls that are in-depth product demonstrations, your presentation is set up to fail if the audience doesn't know why they're there.

- **Losing all sense of time:** Even good presenters struggle with this, because you're on a different plane of existence while presenting. You're running on adrenaline, and you want to get to the end. The audience is running on weak office coffee, and they want to get to a bathroom.

- **Over-reliance on prepared materials:** Instead of speaking to or with you, the presenter zeroes in on some random point in the space-time continuum. It feels focused to the presenter, but to you it looks like a zombie speaking in monotone to no one in particular.

People don't like most presentations because they don't seem important or relevant, take up too much of their time, and bore them with an uninteresting delivery. Good news for you: These can be fixed by addressing the common root problem—the presentation was designed without considering the audience.

Why?

That's certainly the question your audience is asking. Why must I listen to this? Why is it going on and on forever? Why is this person such a bore?

It's not a bad idea if *you* ask that of yourself before you start. Why do a presentation? A presentation:

- Emphasizes or summarizes key pieces of information already provided through a written medium.

- Economizes time to disseminate important information to the largest relevant audience.

- Engages the full sensory experience to help retain information.

When you understand why you're doing a presentation, you begin to understand what good presentations do (or don't do). A good presentation:

- Does NOT cover every detail of a topic and is not an exhaustive, deep-dive into a topic. It IS an action-oriented medium to provide a thesis, key points, and next steps. Your audience should walk away knowing your main idea and what to do with it, and barring that, where to go for additional information.

- Does fit in an average attention span of five-fifteen minutes for introductory topics and forty-five minutes to an hour relevant topics of established interest. That's not to say engagement has to stop there and everyone has to go home. But you should STOP to get feedback, answer questions, and allow a break. Sure, you can break this rule, as many do, just to "go over one more quick thing," but it doesn't matter—they're no longer listening.

- Does NOT merely rely on spoken words that could just as easily be read, just as you're doing, from a slide deck. It DOES engage sight and sound in more compelling ways, and even smell, taste, and touch where applicable. You're trying to turn on the other channels through which people absorb and retain. The more neurons that fire, the better.

The One Thing

You can use the elements of good writing to sharpen a presentation, and get a really great handle on the "why?" of a presentation to avoid the major pitfalls. This is a wonderful start. But it won't make you a great speaker.

You see, it's really one thing, and only one thing, that separates an adequate, C-minus presentation from an A-plus one. If you have it, and develop it, you will stand out as a star, and your ability to present will have a direct effect on your personal and career success. Without it, you'll get by at company meetings and such, but you'll get the same one-and-a-half percent annual cost of living raise as every other "meets expectations" employee.

If you have the one thing, you will be a better presenter in:

- One-on-one settings like introductory meetings or interviews. You'll be remembered when your competition is forgotten.

- Small group dynamics. You'll be seen as the natural leader of the team.

- Formal presentations to large audiences. You'll be thought of as an expert, authority, and a future "go-to" resource.

It's that powerful. Notably, it will even increase the fudge-factor for other technical mistakes you might make with the advice I've given. I can't tell you exactly how to get it, only that you need it. What is it? ***Personality.***

Your personality needs to make the audience feel something, preferably to simply *like* you and/or respect you. Barring all else, even feeling a sense of dislike or irritation is better than feeling nothing at all. (The opposite of love is not hate! It's apathy!) This is why you see good presenters use elements like humor. But anyone can tell a joke. The best presenters don't run away from having a style. Word choice, folksy aphorisms, style of dress, body language—a good presenter knows that he or she must connect with the audience, and that is the basic skill of connecting with people. If you can do that, it doesn't matter if it's one, five, or fifty thousand people. Now, I can't help you grow a personality, but if you've learned anything so far, you might understand that its starts with the directive to:

Be Deliberate

And, as always, you're building one new skill on top of another. Your personality won't be mine, and it shouldn't be. But if you work from first principles, it won't be unnatural, either. The personality you bring to a live presentation is an offshoot of your personal brand that you've established around your authentic self and mutual value. It will come from an informed understanding of value exchange through finance and the credibility of established capital, as well as understanding how to negotiate to others' perception of value. It captures attention, builds interest, empowers decisions, and motivates action just as good writing.

Personality is about knowing who you are and connecting with what people want. That's the thread that runs through the entirety of what I teach. Your personality will shine when you aren't getting tripped up in details. Having the details come second nature will inspire confidence, and a confident personality will reduce the perception of risk, the key to value that we've already identified.

Your competence in front of another person or persons, of any number, really boils down to no more than a) whether they like you and b) whether they are confident you won't screw things up for them. It's just how they feel. Granted, I've seen some people emphasize one area over the other fairly successfully. Some work more on being likable but wing the confidence-inspiring details. Others are a bit rough around the edges, but imbue the sense that they really know their sh*t. I leave it to you to find your own balance, but unless you consider yourself top percentile in either, it's just mathematically safer to work on both.

Summing It Up

- The first principles of good writing apply to speaking. Clarity, relevance, and respect for the audience's time matter.

- Bad presentations lack purpose, go too long, and cram in lots of details the speaker struggles to remember.

- To overcome the pitfalls of presenting, be able to answer clearly "Why." The point is to emphasize, economize, and engage!

- Good presentations focus less on background and more on action, staying brief and activate more senses than listening to words.

- Great speakers are known for their personalities. Focus on likability and competence—it increases your perceived value.

6 TECHNICAL MASTERY

There are two kinds of technical mastery. The first is developing a deep understanding of your primary career field. In my experience, people are usually good at this. Between school, work experience, and industry associations, I find that most people who would describe themselves as a "professional" have a solid grasp of their work and work product. Kudos! That saves me a lot of time, because I don't need to tell you how to be competent in your job. But there's another layer, or layers, depending on how you look at it. This area of technical mastery is in using tools and having ancillary knowledge that adds to your primary skill-set. This is tricky, but super valuable.

Take what you are learning in this book as one example. In addition to your primary job function, you're gaining a functional understanding of sales and marketing. Some have referred to this concept as "skill-stacking." I never had a word at all for it, just an understanding that the more you have to offer, the more differentiated you are. I'm somewhat the reverse of many of you reading this. I have a core expertise in sales, marketing, and communications. In different roles over time, I added to that a working mastery of whatever field in which I happened to be—manufacturing automation, logistics, healthcare IT and billing, etc. Having a lot of engineering coursework under my belt helped. Knowing communications and being highly technical have always been of great value, because so many people lean hard to one side of that spectrum. It's sort of like being a translator. A functional bi-lingual translator is often of higher value than an expert in either respective language.

One could, I suppose, still argue this is merely further refinement of the niche and value proposition of one's primary expertise. Maybe. I don't care how you categorize it. You should always think about, especially in the branding process we discussed, how you could authentically connect with the greatest possible intersection of mutual value. You can have non-related skill-sets that still help you connect with your target tribe. Maybe you're a lawyer who's really into shooting sports. You could use your knowledge of both to a) connect with a tribe based on a common value and b) specialize in legal issues related to firearms ownership. Skill-stack. Specialization. Niche. Whatever.

Still, you cannot claim technical mastery if using the tools of the trade eludes you. I met kids like that in engineering school—could solve complex calculus, couldn't read a blueprint. Worse, I've met 40ish-50ish professionals who avoided ever really learning Microsoft Office because they could always hand it off to someone else. Always, that is, until a client needed something after hours, and said professional opened a blank Word, Excel, or PowerPoint document; experienced hot flashes and a slight seizure; and started hacking at the keyboard like a drunken monkey.

Unfortunately, I don't know all the tools relevant to your job. You'll need a lot of other instruction, time, and materials to get where you need to be if you haven't already achieved it. What I can guide you in is the strategic importance of taking a business view of your success and becoming a CEO of Self. All businesses buy and train on relevant tools. So should you. I provide you the cautionary tale of seasoned professionals I've seen who find themselves first lost, then bitter and angry, that their lack of competence with basic tools sidelines their growth and gets them on the "Strategic Reduction In Force" short list. Don't get canned because your pride got in the way of learning something new.

A Few Basics

I don't know all the tools you need to know, but I can tell you a few basics that have helped me and that will set you apart from the very average folks you work with daily.

Word

Your peers mostly treat Microsoft Word as the world's most expensive electric typewriter. They put the words on the page, then rough format the document by repeatedly hitting the Enter key and/or Spacebar. That gets them by on a one-pager, but it's really frustrating when they have an actual document. Now laid out across multiple pages, every fix on one page seems like it moves something that screws up the next one up. Worse, they need to add a picture or chart, and everything goes all to Hell.

Thankfully, not only are there useful settings for these formatting issues, but you can quickly and repeatably apply them across the entire document. There are "Styles" for which you can not only apply a specific font and size for different types of text—body, headings, bullet points, etc.—but you can also set how much of a space following each paragraph and set indentations consistently. One thing I implore you: If you absolutely can't get the hang of this, don't fake the formatting with spaces and returns. You're just making it harder on whoever fixes your work. Getting the words on the page and no more is better than creating problems they have to clean up.

But seriously, there isn't a reason for you not to go to the local office supply store and buy a "Dummies" book on the topic and become competent.

Excel

Okay, so it's not *my* strongest skill, either. But I do know how to enter formulas, work across multiple sheets in a workbook, and use spreadsheets as basic automation tools such as calculators for specific, repeatable operations or acquire and organize information for a mail merge. Consider that a bare minimum just to make your own life easier. If you're in a position where it's used often, get better!

PowerPoint

Most of the advice about MS Word applies here, and there is something called a "Slide Master" where you can adjust the format of specific slides down to fonts and bullet styles. Like Word, even if you are unfamiliar with these intermediate formatting tools, at least do the courtesy of not doing a lot of manual attempts at formatting. It makes formatting Hell for the poor, underpaid associate cleaning up your mess.

But mostly, don't just write your entire presentation on slides and read it aloud or do lots of goofy sounds or animations.

HTML

HTML isn't code, per se. It is the instruction language for how a browser displays a webpage. Twenty years ago, even professional, top-tier web pages were often manually cobbled together just by writing out the pages in HTML, with a little help from scripts. Today, there's high-end custom software, or even free page builders for amateurs. Still, it can be frustrating to get something to display exactly right or insert customizations. A little rudimentary knowledge of HTML goes a long way, at least in knowing how pages are structured and how things are displayed. Trying to get a color on the page to match exactly your company logo colors? Look up the Hexadecimal conversion for the given **RGB**, **CMYK**, or **Pantone** color, and edit the Hex value in the HTML. Honestly, the need to know HTML is sort of like needing to know how to drive a manual transmission car. It's all but obsolete, and it won't break you not to know. But if you do know, you almost certainly have a better technical understanding of why things work the way that they do, and can look like a smooth operator in a pinch.

Search

This one has made me a hero, guru, or mystic more times than I can count. For most, Google is still the go-to search, but most of the techniques carry to other search engines.

Most people search a word or phrase and call it a day. Then, they get 386,294 results. The top results are always those with the deepest pockets to show up there, either as a paid ad or via SEO (Search Engine Optimization) consultants. This makes it hard to find useful stuff.

Two key points. First, quotes around a term or phrase returns exact matches—the result must contain the word or phrase exactly. Second, the asterisk (*) is a wildcard operator. This is something you can use with the quotation marks to find things you're almost certain of, but not exactly. For example, let's say you're trying to find employee email addresses at a company you'd like to work, and you know their website is "acme.com." To return possible email addresses, search:

"*@acme.com"

The results have to be in that format, with "@acme.com," but will return ANY example of any result in place of the asterisk. You might get "bobd@acme.com" and "janes@acme.com" and "williac@acme.com." From that, I can see that most emails at the company appear to begin with what are presumably a first name and a last initial. But, from the last in the group, it also seems the user name is limited to eight characters, truncating the last letter of "William." But, you're not interested in reaching them; rather you want to contact a department manager, Elizabeth Jackson, about a job. Then, you can try her presumed email address as an exact match search and see if it appears anywhere:

"elizabej@acme.com"

Uh oh. Nothing comes back. Well, maybe that's not her address, or maybe she's just good at keeping off the web. However, there is some precedent from Bob D. that she might use a nickname. You can try "bethj," "lizj," or a number of other variants. Worst case, stick them all in the

"BCC" field on an email with your own address in the "To" field and see what happens!

Mostly, Search is a very logical thing, so the more logically you can think, the better. Take snippets of information you comb and combine with the primary search term or phrase. With basic knowledge and practice, you can be a mystic, too!

Be Deliberate

I've covered some basic skills that will up your professional game—the same skills that are relevant to any business, because you're thinking like a business. That's a solid, strategic first step. Whatever you know as a primary skill, you now know how to use tools not just to be more efficient, but also to better *sell* your ability. Product plus sales equals business!

Still, I can't anticipate all the relevant technical skills you might add on to your core competency to solidify your brand and add more value. And, I *won't* tell you that more is necessarily better. Add too many technical skills or skill combinations, and you look like a generalist or someone destined always to be the assistant. Don't dilute your brand; build your brand!

The skills that you should consider adding to your stack:

- Allow you to be more independent, accomplishing more in less time without the need to procure additional resources to get the job done.

- Make you a "miracle worker." There's a joke of *Star Trek* lore that Chief Engineer Scotty is known as a miracle worker because he always multiplies his repair estimates by a factor of four. You don't need to do that, but having a skill that few have that becomes useful in a crunch situation can make you a hero.

- Seem interesting to others. Not every skill has to relate to your work directly. If it adds appeal and interest to you personally and accentuates your brand, it could work. Not to put too fine a point on it, but a skill or talent that makes you more likeable and authentic is good.

These things all reduce your perceived downside (resource allocation, time drain, chance of failure) and increase your perceived upside (efficiency, versatility, adaptability, and likability). You now know what that means: ***value***.

Summing It Up

- It's a given that you should develop technical competence in your field, but also acquire ancillary skills around tools and other knowledge that fits your brand and adds perceived value.

- In addition to learning specific technical tools, such as software, that relate to your industry, focus on business tools like MS Office and Internet skills that allow you to function more independently, as a business of one.

- Don't try to become a generalist in everything you touch. Instead, focus on things that increase your capacity, problem-solving ability, and add interest to your authentic story and brand.

7 PROCESS & MANAGEMENT

You've done it. In the boardroom of self-reflection, your Marketing, Finance, Legal, Public Relations, Sales, and IT departments all have a solid strategy, and they have broken down internal barriers to work together seamlessly so that Self, Inc. is viewed as the up-and-coming player in your space. Great! But what counts is where you stand at the end of the quarter. And the quarter after. And the one after that. And . . . well, when *can* you say you've succeeded?

Business is often a very goal-oriented endeavor. Quotas. Guidance. Projections. Numbers. The beauty is that it's objective. You win or you lose. That's also the problem. Every moment that you haven't won, you're losing. And even if you reach the point you can call a win, you start back as a loser next cycle. Psychologically, this can be very defeating. I'd argue that's the biggest problem with "how-to" materials that are goals-based. Most people can't stand the stench of their personal failure in working their way to what some external authority calls success.

But there's another HUGE problem. Even if your ego can stand every day in life that you fall short of your goals to bask in glory when you (for a brief moment) reach them—there just aren't enough data points to measure yourself to know you're on track to reaching your goals. In sales, it's typical to have an annual quota—one big goal. But by March, how do you know if you're on track? Do you divide the annual quota by twelve for a monthly view? Or even by four for a quarterly? Honestly, most people in business do, although it doesn't accomplish much. Very few businesses are completely linear. There's an element of seasonality, sometimes slight but others very pronounced. It's easy to think you're doing worse, or even much better, than you really are.

That leads some to insightfully question the validity of managing to goals, whether from a business perspective or a personal development one. I applaud their willingness to buck the status quo. Still, you can focus on process and systems, but how do you design them if not to some objective? And how do you define a process other than a series of micro-goals?

In writing, I talked about the idea of "Rules are for the guidance of the wise and the adherence of fools." The same can be said of goals. What's important is defining what that objective really means to you. Is it really your goal to "Lose 30 pounds" or "Make six figures by time I'm 30" or "Visit Europe before I'm 40?" Or rather, are these a series of negotiations that we engage in with ourselves for ulterior motives? Just as in negotiating with others, as we learned, sometimes people *say* one thing because they're afraid that what they *mean* comes across as unworthy of their investment in it.

"Losing 30 pounds" might mean someone wants to be healthier. And they probably do. But if you think that comes ahead of "Want to be seen as attractive and powerful," you should probably reread a couple of chapters. We're all different, but a lot more the same than anyone likes to admit. You *do* care what at least *some* people think. And you want success of some sort, the value of which we measure in money or achievement. But what does that mean to you? It could represent freedom or validation from others or being what you believe to be the highest form of yourself. A lot of business literature focuses on the idea of specific goals, and this has been translated to mean finite numbers and ideas. However, I would argue that it is more "specific" to go to the broadest level of why the objective is meaningful to you. Own what matters.

As for the day-to-day, the data-driven goal set loves their numbers there, too. Again, I get it; you objectively either did or didn't meet them. Real-life sales is replete with examples, such as daily call or meeting quotas. Better get your 80 phone calls or six on-site meetings! Having managed sales (as well as having been managed), I know what such finite goals as these look like in real life. Plow through 65 smile-'n-dial calls where you're sure a voicemail will pick up so you actually have time to have real conversations with 15 people and do the necessary legwork. Or worse, you avoid accounts that might be great prospects, because the buyer is a Chatty Cathy. Maybe drive to one on-fire prospect, spending the morning on-site, but then dropping off brochures cold at five other places to put them on the call report. In other words, do unimportant things to hit an arbitrary number, and avoid important things that might be good long-term, but which interfere with the short-term.

What's actually important is consistency of activity that is based in the first principles of selling: You must identify people to talk to, talk to them, propose solutions to their problems, and close deals. You can come up with rough numbers that guide you in doing so, but you can't be a slave to the number at the expense of the principle. So it is with your new, business-oriented approach to personal power and influence.

The Big Picture

The overarching theme of this book is strategy over tactics—tactics are too specific to your situation for me to offer direct guidance. At their core, processes are tactics. Through each chapter, I've gotten about as specific into workable processes as one really can without defining your resources and desires.

For every area we've covered, the beginning is ALWAYS "What do I want? On branding: What do you want to convey? On finance: What money and situation do you want? On Negotiation: What do you want? Keep going . . . If you can't define what you want the result to look like, it's hard to get there.

Once you know *what*, you can construct *how* as a series of ongoing steps that must happen. And when you look at each step, ask *why* it matters. If you can't answer why it's directly relevant to the outcome, don't do it. Remember, too, that your big picture result is not a singularity. When you are specific to a result's meaning to you, that meaning is something that must be sustainable over time. Let's face it; there is a difference of process when you think of a one-off, time-based goal like "Lose x pounds" or "Make y dollars." Once you reach a singular point of the intersection of a numerical value at a point in time, what you did to get there is often not related to what's required to maintain it across time.

You may have heard "Begin with the end in mind," but it takes a different shape when you approach things as having no end. Being happier or having more freedom or more choices or being more attractive or having more confidence are not one-and-done things. The bad news is that you'll always be working. The good news is that the work is much more forgiving than holding yourself to a temporary yet unsustainable standard of "goal achievement." Instead, I like the adage, "Act with purpose." Do more of the things that bear a connection to your purpose—what you want. Do less of the things that have no relation to that.

Measure Across Points

It's important to measure progress, but tougher to measure what matters in a meaningful way. People tend to either focus too much on measuring one dimension too frequently, misjudging that they're not making progress. Or, they collect myriad data points as if it's all importing, without real thought towards exactly what they're measuring. "Data-driven" seems to be the popular phrase, and in business, you've likely heard the term "Big Data." The idea is that you can divine meaningful information from a slew of automatically collected data points.

The folks who are into incessant checking of a single point tend to be the goal obsessed. Is the bank account up? Is the bathroom scale down? What did I accomplish today? That might give you good news, bad news that seems more significant than it is, or most likely, simply an incomplete and inaccurate picture. On the other hand, the "Big Data" thinkers tend to see lots of clouds that happen to look like bunny rabbits—as in if you stare an incongruent nonsense long enough, your brain plays a game of trying to see a pattern that doesn't exist as if staring into the sky.

You must connect the action to the intended result. Typically, a series of actions are part of an operation, so catalog each. Also, think about what the result looks like, in detail. The more you picture it in your mind, the more you realize no one attribute defines it. Any life you want to live, from a personal development or business aspect, has multiple dimensions. Actually try to picture it in your mind with all your senses. See yourself in that future state. Then describe it. That's your window to what to measure.

In fact, the "secret" of visualization is the subject of many writings on success, some more mundane and others more divinely inspired, bordering on the supernatural. Either way, it has a great track record of success, whether your brain is connecting to the great beyond to create a solution or whether you've simply trained your brain to focus on what matters and identify patterns that match the vision. It doesn't matter. The more detailed the vision, the more of a blueprint it becomes with finite measurements that you can break down to the most fundamental level of action.

Be Deliberate

At this stage, you have fundamental strategies for bridging your internalized vision to the external world. You have a brand and an understanding of the exchange of value through finance. You understand how those relate to negotiating with others and using writing and presentation skills to reinforce that. You have a core competency and an understanding of tools that make you more efficient.

What remains is putting that to work toward your vision and intended result. You will manage not just yourself but also your interaction with the outside world. You will achieve what you need and your vision by showcasing and providing value. It's a closed loop system. Any of these skills is independently useful, but the point is to use each function together towards your objective.

You might fall short in executing any one area. You may find as you go that your vision changes. But you're managing to a system that minimizes single failures and lets you adapt to changes. That's what a business does, guided by a CEO. See yourself as the CEO and yourself as a business of one in all things, and you can't help but to act with purpose.

Summing It Up

- Don't be a slave to a quantitative goal—it's no more than a point of guidance in achieving a qualitative result across time.

- See the big picture of what the intended result is, and think about it in detail. Think about it in terms of consistent activities to achieve it.

- Don't get bogged in minutia of infinite data points. Purposefully select what to measure in the multiple dimensions of the intended result.

- Use your knowledge and skill in connecting with others to build your vision acting as the CEO of a business of one. Move with purpose and integrate each area of your knowledge in a way that furthers your vision in a way you can measure and/or adjust.

8 REAL LIFE

"Cool story, bro."

That's internet parlance for "You're full of sh*t." And some of you may think so. As they also say, "Show the receipts!" If I'm not an example of what I'm teaching, what I'm teaching is garbage. Am I perfect? Not by any means. Strategic approaches never are—you meet the real world variables later. Strategy doesn't negate the need for tactical execution; it just gives you some breathing room to adjust.

Everything for me comes down to freedom—personal, professional, and political. I accept freedom as nature's design, intended to be humanity's default state. It's not only integral to my brand and building my external tribe; it's the objective that defines my strategies: Have more freedom. The keys to freedom, on any of these levels I've described, are essentially the same:

- Trust - The more ability you show to handle things without screwing them up for someone else, the more latitude you have.

- Respect - Ask no more than you're willing to give, and the more you find others are willing to give.

- Leadership - Freedom means taking responsibility. Take the initiative, and you have the power of choice.

- Competence - Vital in establishing trust, respect, and leadership, but also your currency to walk away and seek mutual value.

- Courage - When what you've given isn't returned in kind, you have to push back. Earn your way, and fight for it when needed.

I build those fundamentals into each of my strategies in this book. But more than that, I've built them into my life. I thought it fitting to offer some examples of what I've been able to accomplish.

Brand

"Hi!" she said, as she broadly smiled and stuck out her hand to shake mine. I grasped it firmly and responded with a hello. She continued, "I just wanted to be the first to greet the new student teacher and wish you luck on your first day!"

That was senior year of high school. It was also not an isolated incident. Early on, I realized dressing a level up brings you near instant credibility in any situation. Look the part—it's the easiest thing you can do. But you need to be able to act the part. Nearly six years later, I was nearing the end of my first year in my first career-level job. I'd had an emergency medical situation on an outing that summer. A swarm of yellow jackets put an early end to a fishing trip in a remote mountain town, and I found myself at their local ER. . . which unlike most colloquial uses of "ER," it literally seemed to be a single room. After a nurse took my vitals, and being still under my own power, they sent me to their clinic across the street because a car accident had the ER completely booked. Instead of billing my insurance as an emergency visit, this resulted in being billed simply as visiting an out-of-network doctor, for which my insurance wouldn't pay.

After weeks of phone calls, voice mails, and e-mails, I finally worked my way up to the C-suite at the hospital system, explaining that their billing error was costing me, asking that they resubmit it as an emergency visit. In talking to this executive, who explained rules about how he couldn't simply change the coding, he offered simply to write me a check for the difference.

"I'm sure you understand, and I appreciate that you've been patient with my team. It sounds like you also manage quite a few employees, yourself! It's not anything intentional; they're just following the rules. But we want to make this right."

I did explain that, at that time, I was literally the most junior member of my office. But, I, consistent with my brand, acted like senior management. I negotiated and wrote in a way that reflected that. And, I took responsibility for the value of the money and methodically worked through the system to find who could help me. My "Brand" earned me the right to connect with someone who could actually help, and wanted to help who he deemed to be a peer. You don't need a title or a credential to start being whom you want to be *today*, and to earn the trust and respect that comes from it.

* * *

Years later, when I made an official transition into management, it was a mere formality. I looked the part. Even in an office with a dress code, someone is always passive-aggressively pushing on it and seemingly getting away with it. *Pas*sive-aggressive gets *pass*ed over. I'd also built trust and respect, demonstrated leadership and competence, and had the courage to step up for what I wanted. You know what that does across time? It makes the perceived downside risk of working with you seem less. And as you now understand, lower perceived risk equals higher perceived value.

Finance

When I graduated college, I was in one of the most enviable financial positions of any college graduate. It took a lot of work and a lot of saving. Tens, maybe hundreds, of thousands of dollars ahead of many others, I credit this financial foundation for much of my subsequent success . . . .

I was broke.

If you think "busted" is bad, don't forget that numbers go endlessly in both directions. Compared to an average loan balance of just under $40,000, it was essentially having $40,000 these debtors did not. I not only saved the loan interest, but I had the opportunity to put my money into things that earned more. More money in investments. More money to put down in cash on other purchases to avoid consumer debt. Just more money.

It always takes more money to get out of a hole than the immediate value of what put you in it, and student loans are a good example. Interest is one component, but opportunity cost and lost purchasing power are less frequently considered other components. Sometimes, things work out where the borrowed money is a successful speculative investment. If you take on debt that allows you an opportunity you otherwise would not have had, that could be smart. However, most people who *think* they're doing that are rationalizing. For that to be true, your future title needs to be something like "Doctor" or "Your Honor" or "Mr. President," and your current state needs to be something like "Working full time just to pay rent and eat, while going to school part time." That's not the average kid going to college straight out of high school to go get an office cube job. In a world where it's of dubious value even to go to college in such a situation, it's *definitely* not worth taking on one thin dime's worth of debt.

It's the fact that I started debt free that has enabled me to leverage fairly average positions into significant raises and promotions, mostly through changing jobs. Specifically, it allowed me to take risks most people either could not, or simply would not. In fact, it materially reduced the risk. Any poker player knows the difference between a winning bluff and actually holding winning cards. A solid, cash-positive bank balance isn't just pocket aces in terms of a safety net; it tangibly increases your confidence in terms of your brand, capital, and negotiating position. Once again, each strategy reinforces the other when you begin and act with greater purpose.

Negotiation

When you negotiate professionally, it can almost seem routine. There's very little I won't negotiate, from purchases to business deals. I've been through sales and mediation trainings on the topic. As I talked about in the chapter on negotiation, many people focus on extolling the upside rather than mitigating the downside in creating an equation of perceived value. However, there's one other twist that's benefitted me on many occasions, and that is removing the perceived upside of the other person's default course of action. In other words, take "do nothing" or "path of least resistance" off the table by making the costs suddenly tangible.

I was doing some contract sales and marketing work for a small business years ago who found themselves in the unfortunate position of owing their vendors a lot of money because an employee had illicitly put personal purchases on the company account, referencing client jobs on the Purchase Order (PO) as cover. This is the kind of petty crime that almost always gets discovered, but not before a lot of damage is done. The company quickly found itself owing the vendors more than they could pay, unable to pass it on to their clients. Substantial time would be needed to recoup the loss through legal action against the employee. If you've ever owned any type of small business, you know that cash flow is one of the biggest problems there is, even when everything is going great. You have people to pay while you're waiting to be paid. Also, you can't simply slow-pay your vendors as some clients will do to you, because you purchase from them on an ongoing, day-to-day basis.

So you can imagine, a situational crisis can not only grind business to a halt, tempers can flare. Right away, the vendor placed liens on the clients referenced in each PO. Almost anyone can place a lien on anybody else for about any reason. This spurred angry calls from clients to the company, who felt their property was compromised. Exasperated, the company owner asked me to call the vendor.

The first thing I did? I expressed my understanding and regret and let the vendor talk. They were rightfully frustrated, so why take that away? They'd always let the company procure what they needed on a PO without cash up front, and they felt like they were getting screwed—because they were. Unfortunately, they couldn't squeeze blood from a turnip. Their power move of intimidating company clients would quickly have a ripple effect. Word of mouth would halt the ability to sell any new jobs, to say nothing of collecting outstanding payments from clients who'd just been liened. The vendor couldn't see it, but they were in their own way. I needed to show them.

"Look, I understand. You want to get paid. I want you to be paid. But we can't pay you with money we don't have. And calling our clients ensures we're won't have any money to pay you. So please, stop calling them, and we'll work it out."

Angry people don't always get the appeal of simple "If A, then B" logic. And he was angry. "I don't care what you want. We'll stop calling them when you pay us."

"I see. You'd like to be paid sooner. Not later."

"That's right."

"Okay, well, I'm not a lawyer. I don't even own the company. But if you keep calling our clients, then the owner has no choice but to involve the lawyers. And, again, I'm not a lawyer, but I'm sure you'll *eventually* win. A long time from now. So, you'll be paid. A very, very long time from now. You get paid either way, sooner or later, but you need to stop liening and calling our clients if you want it to be sooner."

"Is that a threat?"

"No, sir. It's a choice. Let me know whether you would like this worked out now through us or later through the lawyers. I'm good either way."

He chose the former. The upside of his first approach died, because I understood his need and made the cost of staying the course too high. With him backing off and the thieving employee caught red-handed, in real legal trouble, the owner was able to work out having him replay what he'd taken.

Always let the other person "decide." Just reframe the choices.

Writing

People fight against writing, and I don't know why. You don't have to be great, only better than average. And average is so bad, that you could put in just a little work to be decent. I've heard of writing referred to as a superpower, because it damn near is. While the other kids were choosing the multiple-choice section of the test in lieu of submitting an essay answer, I was earning an "A+" and finishing early. Today, I consider a blank page and a blank check to be about the same, just waiting for me to fill in what I hope to take to the bank.

While I've written six and even seven or eight figure sales proposals in my work, the most immediate memories of cashing a piece of writing are the business letters I've done on my own behalf or a friend's in arguing for my or their interests. A few years ago, I wrote to the president of an outdoor products company about an item of theirs that fell apart while I was fishing. Sure, it was out of warranty, but the company had a reputation of long-lasting, quality products. That I took the time to find the right person (the president) and write a letter referencing how disappointed I was in light of their reputation resulted in getting a check for the amount of the product, about $75.

I did the same for a friend whose front fender was scratched by an auto parts store installing a battery. These kinds of things are routine—store offers a service as a value-add, but doesn't bother to pay qualified people to do the work. The car wasn't new, so most people don't want to bother with insurance or a body shop for a scratch. But at the same time, the damage is real and matters. You could file in small claims court, but between the filing fee and time involved, everyone comes out a loser. This, again, is where a well-written letter to the right person is the winning approach. Find the store's district manager whose job it is to make problems go away. Send a letter. Get paid. Buff out the scratch the best you can and pocket about $400.

Some years later dealing with a property management company after frozen pipes caused water damage, I was more than three weeks in to what should have been three days worth of repairs, waiting on their select, low-bidder vendors to schedule work. Another letter, another roughly $700 to cover loss of use.

That's nearly $1200 in just in off-the-top-of-my-head, random examples. But I can't begin to calculate the total real value. This kind of no-nonsense business writing skill will add value to any kind of work you do. I've recouped probably tens of thousands from vendors who didn't deliver, and it added to my value as an employee. With a business letter, you can:

- Prospect for clients

- Propose new business
- Recoup losses from vendors
- Defend against complaints

If you like making money and keeping more of it, learn to express concise arguments and facts in compelling writing. Let it replace yelling, threatening, bickering, avoiding, and getting railroaded.

Presentation

As mentioned in the chapter on the subject, personality is what sets apart great speakers. For better or worse, your personality when you present is what you will be seen as by others long after it is over. Dull, nervous, pedantic, low-value presenters usually end up being perceived as dull, nervous, pedantic, and low-value. But, fun, knowledgeable, and dynamic presenters are seen as fun, knowledgeable, and dynamic. People want more of that. Thus, they want more of *you* if you can provide that.

I worked at a company where a formal presentation was part of the interview process. Then, in my first week on the job, there was a department-wide training in which I had to do another presentation. I was without the benefit my peers had in already being familiar with the company, market, and solutions. Either presentation could have sunk me—in neither case was it possible for me to be the most knowledgeable about the things they knew. I had to be me. I had to reframe myself as the expert in *my* areas of competency, not be an also-ran by trying to fit precisely in to their world.

I didn't have the advantage as a technical expert in their field, so I presented as the sales expert. Present what you know. Try to stray into being what you're not, and you have a room full of people ready to call your bluff. Besides, if I'm just another one of them, what gives me the right to stand in the front of the room? By highlighting what was unique about me, both in specific knowledge and personality, I earned the credibility to stand in front of the room and be considered as a peer from then on. (Different but equivalent expertise is still a peer-to-peer relationship.)

Technical Mastery

Layered skills not only multiply value, they add freedom. Whatever you can do directly in one less thing for which you must depend on others. These skills can either make money directly, earn more for your primary area of competency, or save you time and money.

Or, you can be the counterexample, which perhaps is a more meaningful reminder of why you shouldn't ignore the things that will make you more well rounded. I, and probably you, have had more bosses than I can count who could not do the things I could. On one hand, you could look at that as how they had more money and authority than I without the benefit of these skills. On the other, I wouldn't be able to tolerate the absolute bind they were in, because they had no freedom. They depended on their employees to look good, which also put them in the position that their employees could make them look bad. They were in a constant state of fear-motivation, adrift in the sea of things outside their control.

Sometimes, you meet someone who hasn't kept up with the changing landscape yet has the self-awareness to realize it.

"Are you good with Excel, Jared?"

I answered, "I'm okay. I'm not as strong with it as Word or PowerPoint."

She looked at me knowingly and said, "Then you'll want to get good at it."

These were wise words from one of my greatest managers, a senior-level VP who only in her 40s was at the top of her game, respected industry-wide, and earning probably a half million a year. And, oh, by the way, she was a disaster with technology! She routinely carried around reams of handwritten notes. Her directive to me was not one of arrogant superiority. It was a caution from a high-achiever who possessed the self-awareness to see that you can always be better than you are, and that taking solid strategic knowledge and putting it with a little tactical know-how can put you in a higher echelon of professionals.

She "retired" from that job a few weeks later, having done well but the grind of change putting her legacy and continued success at risk. Her departure turned it into a truly miserable job for me, fraught with chaos and a lack of vision. But I had no choice but to put layered skills to my advantage—yes, improving with Excel, but also establishing my niche of internet research skills, organizing proposals, managing projects, and maintaining the CRM database. None of these made that job any less miserable, but the résumé boost made the next transition quick and much better!

Process

I need as much as possible to be on autopilot. I don't discount the entire importance of key measures, but I do recognize that if you focus on the quantitative without the qualitative, you obsess over things that ultimately don't matter. And if you focus only on the qualitative without the quantitative, you can fall far short of potential.

In my early 30s, like many of you, I found that the habits of my 20s were manifesting as greatly different physical results. At 6'3", I was over 250 pounds. I didn't look the way I wanted, and I didn't feel like I should. I knew I had to change, but these habits were also built over a lifetime. I also wasn't hung up on a number, but I knew that a few years earlier when I was in the 220s, I felt fine, was active, and my wardrobe worked. I was willing to put in the work. What I was not willing to do is have the administration of the work exceed the effort of the work. Over the next few months, I lost 30 pounds. Let's start with what I didn't do:

- I didn't count calories.
- I didn't weigh daily or have a set number I expect to see weekly.
- I didn't follow or count a set number of reps of any one exercise.
- I didn't throw everything in my kitchen away.
- I didn't totally give up any one kind of food.

Understand, if these things work for you as part of a system, great. None of them worked for me. Too much administration. Too much deprivation. Too much daily thought. But as I read about what doctors and experts recommended, I realized I could experience the benefit of their ideas by setting up systems I could live with and that would just be a part of how I did things.

- I would drink as few calories as possible.
- I would cut out evening snacks.
- I would weigh every week to see progress, not a specific number.
- I would buy healthier options at the store.
- I would exercise for about an hour at least four days a week.
- I would mix cardio and strength training.

Some genius no doubt will critique my methods, that I could have lost more weight or done so more quickly, or that I could have gained more strength or endurance. And my answer is, no, I couldn't have. Because, I simply wouldn't have done it. That's the problem with prescriptive advice. It measures proportionally, optimizing each detail. That doesn't work with a binary challenge: Do something or do nothing. If I couldn't have a simple system that I didn't have to think about and which didn't demoralize me over small failures, I would have simply stayed fat. My way got me *not* fat, which was the objective, and someone else's genius way would have left me fat. So my way works, and theirs is a failure.

Well, for me, that is. It'd be as foolish for me to prescribe my system for you. What I can do is tell you that what you do should be a system so that you can maintain it over a long period of time without bogging down in things you can't control, don't care about, or which are in some way self-defeating.

* * *

All that brings me back to this:

If I can build a life around what's meaningful and authentic . . .

If I can put up six-figures in my bank account . . .

If I can stand up for myself and win . . .

If I can lose 12% of my body weight in a few months . . .

If I can be recognized as uniquely knowledgeable . . .

. . . then you can, too.

I'm not better than you. My advantages weren't unique or great, and to some degree, we all have a mix of advantages and disadvantages. There's nothing special in my story other than what I make of it because of my determination to be the best I can be and live as freely as possible using what I have to work with. What I teach isn't a precise roadmap for you because your destination is your own. But I present my experience as proof that a strategic, first-principles approach will make your trip a lot easier with fewer detours.

AFTERWORD

Although I designed this book to be read in order, I won't fuss if you flipped here first for some clue as to whether you are ready to dig in. Keep reading, and if so inclined, go back to the start. For those of you who made it through to here, I hope these parting thoughts will give you some additional context for reflection on how to use what you've learned.

I've been acknowledged for my professional work in sales and marketing as well as for my political work and advocacy.

This book isn't really either. It is also in some ways both.

The idea of this book is to help you, personally, sharing what I know. I don't build artificial silos around my knowledge, and the product here is the whole of my experience as well as authentic to my own brand as a communicator, persuader, and believer in human potential born of freedom. Still, this isn't a one-size-fits-all prescription for professional success or political proselytizing. I've endeavored to give you the whole of me without diminishing you.

My experience and beliefs simply inform my approach. However, both are firmly grounded in the first-principle ideas that:

- By virtue of our talents and experience, we all know something that others do not.

- The way to help others and benefit society is to pursue individual excellence with our talents and experience, and through our diversity, we create a thriving environment as a more functional, capable whole.

My objective is for you to be the best you can be, using the entirety of what I can offer you, while acknowledging that you come here, now, with talents that I don't have and experiences that are unique to you. Consider this book additive, not subtractive. If it causes you to reframe old assumptions or question something you thought you knew, fine, but the point here has been to offer something anyone, and everyone, can use.

I hope you will use it, because I also believe, based in principle and experience, that the world is undergoing profound change for which past teaching and systems have left most people woefully unprepared. From where I sit, it's the biggest change since the Industrial Revolution, and just as historic and significant. As in that example, the changes will both be wondrous for humanity yet often harsh and unforgiving to the individual. It will both create and destroy.

In some ways, the change will mirror the Industrial Revolution, which saw cottage industries rendered obsolete by mass manufacturing, changing everything from our consumption habits to our educational model. Formal schooling expanded across the 20th Century as apprenticeship and vocational training shrunk. Labor models were built on predictability, thus was everything else feeding into that model. Today, people perform all sorts of jobs without having any understanding of why they do so in eight-hour shifts using education that has little bearing on the job function, which is itself largely interchangeable.

Automation and Artificial Intelligence will as certainly replace some jobs as Model T automobiles replaced the horse and carriage. However, such expansions of human productivity through technology have never capped our long-term economic health—rather they've always grown it. The change will simply cause us to reevaluate whether our work and educational paradigms still make sense. I've not been called a visionary, but I'll go out on a limb and predict that those paradigms will be found lacking, because they've really been hobbling along for at least 50 years disconnected from what drove them.

I foresee a return to the cottage industry, married to the best of the industrial and technological world. What some wring their hands about, fretting, really presents an opportunity not seen in generations:

- The prosperity of the industrial era.

- The individual worth and knowledge of master craftsmen.

- A class mobility unseen in previous eras.

It's exciting, if a little scary. It will, based on history, lead to an increase in health and living standards that have always accompanied economic growth. But it will disrupt accepted norms and temporarily displace those who are unprepared. At the same time, as with such previous shifts in society, it will lead to political upheavals. Some will be healthy, based in recognition of tangible changes and the necessity to address them. Others will be knee-jerk, a reflexive response to what is little understood and unleashing unintended consequences.

Those are broad predictions, but with no one having a crystal ball, all you can do is go back to first-principles. You are in business for yourself, whether you sell to one client or many. For long-term stability, math suggests that it is better to have many clients, although you've been taught the opposite. You have to add value through differentiating yourself and what you offer. You must continue to evolve your offering and update how you market it based on how the marketplace changes.

This gives me room to get some of the details of the vision wrong, which is also the beauty of any worthy system. I want to help you take advantage of these inevitable changes, be more free, enjoy more prosperity, and build a better society. But short of all that, if I simply help you do marginally better in the same life you were already living by finding a little efficiency and greater return on your effort, I still call that a win.

Either way, challenge the status quo and question your assumptions, most all of which has been passed on out of habit rather than reason. Don't depend on parents, connections, schools, or jobs to be able to promise you security. The best way to predict your future is to design it, proactively. That's what this book is really about.

I can't wait to see what you do with it!

ABOUT THE AUTHOR

Jared A. Chambers is a strategic communications consultant and content creator. His practice, Professional Perception, specializes in sales, political advocacy, and personal development; providing training and developing messaging. Prior to this and after earning his degree in Technical Communication from Southern Polytechnic State University, his career spanned more than 15 years in sales, marketing, and management in healthcare and high-tech. Jared lives in his native state of Georgia, enjoying local culture and the outdoors. Follow him on Twitter @C4CEO and connect on LinkedIn at linkedin.com/in/jachambers, or visit www.professionalperception.com.

Made in the USA
Columbia, SC
17 January 2025